Contents

Ada Brownell

CONFESSIONS OF A PENTECOSTAL

Gospel Publishing House
Springfield, Missouri
02-0476

CONFESSIONS OF A PENTECOSTAL
© 1978 by the Gospel Publishing House
Springfield, Missouri 65802

Library of Congress Catalog Card Number 77-92887
International Standard Book Number 0-88243-476-4
Printed in the United States of America

1

Brand-new

Our family didn't like her. She had no tact.

Mom told the lady she wasn't interested in her religion, but the woman didn't seem to care. She came to our house almost every day, her Bible tucked under her arm, an enthusiastic smile on her face.

The family did everything they could to get rid of her. Mom tried to ignore her and would continue her work as if she weren't there. But the old lady would read the Bible and preach to Mother anyway, and she couldn't help but hear.

All Pentecostal people were crazy according to what we had heard. We made fun of the "Holy Rollers" and enjoyed it immensely.

My oldest sister, Marjorie, had a tremendous dislike for the stubborn old woman. But Marjorie wasn't rebellious toward God or church; so when her best friend invited her to attend church with her, she agreed.

"What church do you go to?" Marjorie asked as the two sophomores walked home together.

The girl pointed to the little white church on the corner.

Marjorie's mouth fell open. "You go to *that* church?"

"That" church was an Assemblies of God church located in the center of Fruita, a small community on the western slope in Colorado. Marjorie had called it the "Holy Roller" church ever since our family had moved to Fruita a few months earlier from Kansas. She'd heard quite a bit about "that" church. But now she was confused. She had heard all those people were mentally disturbed, but her friend didn't look or act crazy. Marjorie decided to go and see for herself.

That night Marjorie was nervous, not knowing what to expect. When someone jumped to his feet and began to speak in a language she didn't understand and another person began speaking loudly in English, Marjorie was scared. She ran outside and waited for her friend on the church steps.

Soon another friend invited Marjorie to attend a revival meeting at "that" church. She'd already heard about the revival in progress, as we all had, from the old lady who lived across the street.

"You've got to come to this revival!" the lady kept telling us. "People all over town are getting saved. God's working miracles. You've got to come."

Because of her affection for her new friends, Marjorie tried to forget her first experience and decided to go again.

To Marjorie's horror, her friend led her to the front of the church and sat down on the second row. It would be hard to make a fast getaway from up there!

Marjorie listened to the sermon. It frightened her as much as the unusual praying and speaking in tongues. But soon she was under conviction and no longer felt like making fun. She knew she was a sinner.

Her heart was heavy as she walked the half mile home from the service. She was afraid Jesus would come back to get the "saved" people before she could go to church again and be converted.

When Marjorie went again, she had already made up her mind to get saved. After the altar call was given she knelt and knew she'd had a personal encounter with God. She found joy and peace she'd never known.

Marjorie arrived home that night shining with joy and enthusiasm.

"You've got to get saved!" she began as she told what had happened. Soon her urging became more dynamic. "If you don't get saved, you're going to hell!" Her words were not angry or vengeful but full of compassion, love, and fear for the souls of our family.

Mother was upset. The old lady across the street had been working on her for a long time now, and Mom wasn't so sure she'd been correct when she had said the woman was crazy. Marjorie had changed. She was no longer a rebellious teenager. She was a different person since her conversion.

The old lady kept coming. "You've got to come to this revival!" she said. Mom knew the woman was genuinely excited. She had been going up and down our street and all over town telling people about the meeting.

Mom decided to go just to find out what Marjorie had gotten herself into. Mother was scared too. She listened from the steps the first night, but since she couldn't tell exactly what was going on, she decided to go again so she could see the people worship.

That night Marjorie was seeking for the baptism in the Holy Spirit. One of her friends had received, and Marjorie wanted the experience too.

As soon as she knelt at the altar, the power of God descended upon her and she began to shake as she praised the Lord in a loud voice.

Mother, watching from a distance, came closer. When she saw Marjorie shaking in the presence of God, she thought she was having a nervous relapse from an old spinal injury. Marjorie had fully recovered from that injury, but when Mother saw her shaking at the altar she was certain it had recurred.

"Get her up from there!" she told the altar workers. They ignored her; so Mother got next to Marjorie and tried to calm her down.

But Marjorie felt wonderful. She was in ecstasy. As she rejoiced in the Lord, she became unable to articulate her words and prayed with stammering lips. She thought she had received the baptism in the Holy Spirit. When she got up, however, her friend said, "Don't give up when you're this close."

"You mean I didn't receive?" Marjorie asked. She knelt again and as soon as her knees touched the floor she began speaking in a language she had never learned. God had rewarded her persistence and complete consecration.

A Swedish couple skeptical of Pentecostals was watching the altar service. When Marjorie began speaking in tongues they turned to listen. Afterwards they told the church she had been praising the Lord in Swedish. The couple became Pentecostal believers, along with others who had attended the revival out of curiosity.

After receiving the baptism in the Holy Spirit, Marjorie preached to our family with more fervor than ever.

One by one the older children got saved. Our

neighbors were also getting saved. My father got under conviction and quit smoking. Then he accepted the Lord Jesus Christ as his personal Saviour.

The neighbor woman continued reading the Bible to Mom. Finally Mother realized that the New Testament church was Pentecostal and she too got saved and received the Holy Spirit. As the younger children grew up, they accepted Christ and were filled with the Spirit. As the youngest, I was privileged to grow up in the best Christian home a child could be blessed with.

In our family of eight children there is a minister, Everette D. Nicholson; two Christian college professors, Dr. Virgil Nicholson and Dr. Joe Nicholson, both of Evangel College in Springfield, Missouri; a Christian writer; Sunday school workers; personal evangelists; and Christian parents. We're all Pentecostal.

My own personal encounter with God came when I was about 5 years old. I was looking at the stained-glass windows in the old church the Assembly of God had bought from some other denomination. The pastor was preaching on the second coming of Jesus Christ. Suddenly it looked as if I could see through the windows and Jesus was coming in the sky. The invitation was given and I ran to the altar to accept Him as my personal Saviour.

From that day forward, even as a child, I felt very close to God. I enjoyed feeling the warm, comforting Presence that descended on us time and again at church, at cottage prayer meetings, and even when we prayed as a family at home.

Often when our church was particularly "on fire" for God, sinners would weep when they entered the building; people had prayed so much, the presence of God continually filled the sanctuary, and they could feel God's power just by walking inside.

It was not unusual in those days for people who were afraid to enter the building to stand outside and peer in the windows. Some of them then felt compelled to come in and give their lives to God.

Faith was strong in those days. In fact, I was reared on faith. From the time I was born until I got married I was only examined by a doctor once—when I had a severe case of the croup and the doctor made a house call. We relied on the power of prayer, and doctors were only a last resort to keep Mom, Dad, and the eight of us in health.

We depended on God to supply our needs and we never missed a meal. We feasted on the Word and found going to church enjoyable.

We weren't late often, but I remember one time on a Sunday night when we came in late the congregation was singing jubilantly,

"Yes, I know, I surely know,
Jesus' blood can make the vilest sinner clean. . . ."[1]

Even though I was still a child, the singing sent chills down my spine. *If only the drunks in town knew that! If only the woman who laid down on the railroad tracks near our home and committed suicide had known that! If only the whole world could know that Jesus' blood can make the vilest sinner clean!*

It's been more than 30 years since I accepted Jesus as my Saviour. Am I still enthusiastic about Him? Am I as dedicated? Do I still have faith to rely on God? Is there value to serving Him? Or are there doubts?

---

[1] Anna W. Waterman, "Yes I Know," 20th Century.

2

Baptism of Oil

"Anyone can say gravy over and over, faster and faster, until he gets his tongue mixed up and sounds like he's speaking another language."

The speaker was my best friend. She was a Christian but attended a church that didn't believe in speaking in tongues. She knew and I knew that "gravy," or some other such nonsense, had never been used in Pentecostal churches to tangle a tongue. But I'd seen many who used a "praise" word such as "glory" or "hallelujah" as they waited for the heavenly fire of Pentecost. We always saw it as a way of seeking the Holy Spirit and an easier means of yielding to the Spirit of God, since we didn't have to keep thinking up new phrases as we tarried. We were praising God for the Gift instead of begging for it.

As my friend and I stood outside the church talking, waiting for the revival service to which I'd invited her to begin, I felt an uneasiness stirring inside me. *Perhaps the experience isn't what I've always thought.* I'd been baptized in the Holy Spirit when I was about 9 years old, at a time when speaking in tongues was almost a status symbol among the children of the church. Yet, I'd had many refillings of the experience, and it seemed each refilling was better than the last. The Holy Spirit filled a vacancy that nothing else could satisfy.

But as my friend and I talked about it doubts came. Did Pentecostals really speak in an unknown language or a heavenly language—conversing with God? We were both 15 and I was at the age where I was testing many of the things I'd been taught all my life. Besides, it had been quite a while since I'd spoken in tongues.

It would have been easier to think about my friend's criticism of Pentecostal worship if the church hadn't already been in revival. The familiar warm, comforting sensation of God's presence greeted us as we entered the church. We'd built a new church in Fruita by then, but the Presence was the same.

The presence of God descending on His people is no new phenomenon. The glory of the Lord filled Solomon's Temple at the feast of dedication and it was so powerful that the priests couldn't stand to minister (1 Kings 8:11). God's presence has been with individuals and congregations since Adam.

God's presence in our little church the night I brought my friend seemed especially strong. I don't remember who the evangelist was.

Soon a non-Christian friend I'd invited came in and the three of us sat together. In spite of my friends, as the preacher became anointed during the sermon the familiar warmness of the Holy Spirit was not only on the outside of me, it also was burning within. I had longed for a new touch from God—even before this night.

By the time we stood to praise the Lord, tears were running down my cheeks and I was praising the Lord in tongues loudly enough for my friends to hear. I didn't care what they thought. I didn't care if they thought I was making it up. I didn't care if they thought I was in hysterics or that I was crazy.

In those minutes, it was Jesus and me. Stored-up doubts vanished as I felt Him and conversed with Him in words I'd never been able to say in English. My faith was firm again—on the Rock.

Later my friends said, "It's real. I could feel it. It just flowed out of you. There was nothing fake about that. Now I know why you believe in speaking in tongues."

It was not I who convinced them of the validity of the experience—it was the Holy Spirit. My friends knew me. I was afraid to speak up in school even when I knew the answer. If an instructor asked me a question, panic struck me and I only shrugged my shoulders, indicating he'd better call on someone else.

During that service, however, I spoke loudly enough for the girls to hear—even when I knew they doubted.

My unsaved friend later went to the altar for salvation. The Christian girl who didn't believe in the Holy Spirit's infilling with speaking in tongues didn't seek for the Baptism but she never again criticized it and often attended church with me.

Although I have spoken in tongues nearly every day of my adult life, there seems to be a special anointing that comes with a fresh outpouring—when the "cup" is not only full but overflowing.

Acts 4:31 indicates that the Early Church received a refilling of the Holy Spirit only a few days after Pentecost. The lame man had been healed at the gate of the temple. Because of the uproar the miracle had caused in the city, Peter and John were threatened and told not to speak in Jesus' name again.

Immediately they called a prayer meeting. Luke, the historian, writes: "And when they had prayed, the place was shaken where they were assembled together; and they were all filled with the Holy Ghost, and they spake the word of God with boldness" (Acts 4:31).

When my cup was full and running over, I too began to speak the Word of God with boldness. God began to use my life after that refilling in front of my friends.

When I was 15, God told me I was going to be elected president of the church youth group. (If He hadn't, I'd have been so overwhelmed I'm sure I would have refused to accept the position.) I was nearly the youngest member of the group, which consisted of everyone from 13 to 35. Most of the members were married.

I'd spoken for the group once. God had given me a message about Christians who were dining "banquet-style" on God's riches, while at our very doors people were starving for the message of the Lord Jesus Christ. We weren't even sharing the "crumbs" from our table, as the rich man had done with Lazarus.

I had no idea (until God told me) that I could lead the group. I was so young it seemed preposterous to think that I could lead men and women in their thirties. Yet, I knew God was appointing me. I felt little emotion—only a desire to fulfill God's plan for my life. Already God had given me ideas for services and my heart was hot to begin reaching out and doing something besides having a little "club."

Sure enough, I was elected. Immediately I began spending hours in prayer. I studied the Word. When I was desperate for something, I fasted a meal. Within a few days, the answer usually came.

I wrote letters and cards to everyone I could think of who had shown any interest in the church but hadn't been attending. (One young man must have thought I had a personal interest in him, because he came the very next week after receiving a card. He grinned at me quite nicely until he discovered my interest was in his soul and I already had a boyfriend. The young fellow never did come back.)

In a short time, the services in the youth hall were packed. A few times the power of God was so strong in the meeting that our early service couldn't be dismissed in time for the next service to begin, but we had the pastor's blessings. He rejoiced with us.

During this time I prayed with a number of young people desiring salvation at the altar. I knew the glory was God's. I could see the difference in the effectiveness of the services when I prayed at least an hour on Sunday afternoon.

* * * * *

When I married Les he was a telegraph operator. Soon after our wedding we moved to the top of Tennessee Pass on the Continental Divide where he was an agent for the Rio Grande Railroad. We drove to Minturn to church and we soon became involved with the work there. The church was about 10 years old, and the pastor said that to his knowledge no one had ever received the Holy Spirit in that building.

The pastor's wife, Elaine Nelson, and I agreed to pray for revival and stood on the Scripture passage, "If two of you shall agree on earth as touching any thing that they shall ask, it shall be done for them of my Father which is in heaven" (Matthew 18:19).

After several months revival came. It started with the children, which dismayed many of the adults. They thought their kids were becoming fanatical and that the demonstrations should be stopped. About 20 children, however, received the baptism in the Holy Spirit. (The church attendance was around 60.)

The revival, however, wasn't confined to the children. It soon spread to the adults. New commitments and rededications were made, and people were filled with the Spirit. Others were healed, and we began to believe God for a crippled man's healing. Herman had polio and previously had been a robust railroad engineer. He was broken in spirit as well as body because of what the disease had done to him.

Although Herman didn't throw away his crutches as we had hoped, his broken spirit was healed. He found a job he could do and continued serving God faithfully because he found His grace is sufficient in spite of circumstances. I've discovered that sometimes God is glorified more by the person who, despite disastrous circumstances, serves Him lovingly, faithfully, and totally—than if God performed a miracle.

Even though this revival preceded the charismatic movement, the pastor of the Presbyterian church (who really was a Methodist, if you can understand that) came over every Sunday night to watch our altar services. Many of the adults were on fire for God and people were getting saved, filled with the Holy Spirit, and healed.

In our church was a backslidden minister who had previously been associated with the Spanish Assemblies of God. I've never been able to understand a backslider, so while we were having friendly visits in each others' homes I constantly badgered him about his spiritual condition. I did it in a jesting manner and he'd laugh it off, but he knew I was serious.

"We've got the whole church praying for you," I'd grin. "I don't know how you can stand it! We know you're coming back to the Lord and going back into the ministry, so there's no use fighting it! You haven't got a chance with us and the Lord working on you."

It was almost more than I bargained for, however, when during an altar service the Lord told me to go ask the backslidden preacher to go to the altar. I'd always frowned on women praying with men (and still do, except with their husbands). Yet, the command was so imperative I got up and went to talk to him. His wife was sitting beside him and tears were scurrying down her face.

"Why don't you come back to Him tonight?" I asked gently. I was trembling from head to toe.

"I can't," he protested, sorrow written on his face. "I can't after what I've done."

I didn't bother to inquire what he meant.

"After what *you've* done?" I asked in horror. "What about what *He's* done? That's what Christ died for—sinners. You're going to let all that suffering for you go to waste? He didn't have to die, you know, He *chose* to die for our sins. Nothing you have done could keep Him from taking you back."

By now he was crying. Slowly, he got up, and his wife and I led him to the altar.

Sure enough, a few months later he was back in the ministry. We moved several hundred miles away, but about a year later he and his family stopped to see us. With tears in his eyes he thanked us again for caring—for having enough nerve to speak to him— and leading him back to God.

But the reaping hadn't been my work only. The Holy Spirit is the One who draws men and women to Christ. His family had prayed and longed to see him joyful in the Lord again. And I'm thankful for my husband, who is quiet yet doesn't get embarrassed or harrass me when I witness to someone as I did the backslidden minister. He has always supported and helped me whenever he could. (He also does personal evangelism when the opportunity arises.)

Until we moved to Utah, I saw results of God's power almost daily. The Holy Spirit filled me, thrilled me, satisfied me, and caused me to be instrumental in leading a number of people to the Lord Jesus Christ.

Utah, however, was another experience. Thompson, a desert community where we lived for 5 years, had a population of only about 100. It seemed everyone in town except the children lived for the weekends so they could get drunk. We had four bars and the two grocery stores were located in bars. I was required to go into a bar to get milk and bread.

For several months, we drove the 90 miles to Fruita, Colorado on weekends to stock up on groceries and attend church. The move to Thompson put an abrupt end to my church work.

Only a few weeks after moving to Thompson, two ladies came to visit. They extended friendly greetings, then announced that they had heard I played the piano and wondered if I'd play for the children in the community who were taking tap-dancing lessons.

My heart sank. "I can barely play by notes," I stammered. "I only play church music and, most of the time, I don't really know what I'm doing. I play what I feel and hear. God gave me all the talent I have and I feel I can only use it for Him."

They tried to be gracious, but I knew I'd made a sour introduction into the social life of Thompson.

My guess was correct, for it was a year before anyone said anything to me that he didn't have to. I became very lonely. Between Sundays I usually talked to three people: my husband, my 1-year-old son, and the woman in the post office. I firmly thought I was out of the will of God, but I didn't know what to do about it. At times I was bitter.

"God," I'd pray, "You know I was working for You and had dedicated my life to You. Why do You leave me here in this place, surrounded by sinners? I need a friend. I need fellowship. You said You'd give us the desires of our hearts."

When I mentioned the "desires of our hearts" I envisioned myself living in a suburban neighborhood where I was surrounded by neat houses and green grass (instead of tumbleweeds, dry dirt, and shacks). I envisioned myself attending a large church and working with youth or involved in some other rewarding ministry.

A move, however, didn't come. Les' railroad job was governed by seniority and we were stuck in Thompson. A period of temptation came. One evening Les and I talked it over. Was definite separation from the world really necessary and worth it? We decided that it was.

Les began having to work Sunday mornings, so we drove to Moab, Utah to church on Sunday evenings from then on. Moab was 38 miles away, but we made friends with some fantastic people who were dedicated Christians. Sometimes they'd drive to our house for a meal and fellowship during the week or they'd invite us to come to Moab for dinner and an evening of friendship.

The church in Moab was thriving, but my bitterness at living in Thompson made my soul as dry as stale bread. It seemed every time the pastor preached he'd say, "These are the last days, folks. In the last days there will be a great falling away. The days of revival may be over. But keep hanging in there."

Probably I heard only the negative things. But I had become so dry, instead of fountains of joy, my soul felt pain when I knelt to pray. My speaking in tongues was reduced to a few short syllables at the end of my prayers. I longed and thirsted for the joy of the Lord. Finally, I came to a point of desperation.

"If I don't get a refilling at church soon," I told one of my friends in whom I had confided, "I'm going to get on my knees at home and stay there until I hear from heaven."

The next Sunday I stood up to testify on the platform at church where I'd been playing my accordion in the orchestra. Suddenly as I began to speak, it felt like hot oil was being poured over me. It began on the top of my head and flowed down my body until I felt saturated. I began crying and speaking in tongues. The hot anointing of the Spirit of God was inside me again and the river of joy was undammed.

When the speaking in tongues subsided, I began testifying under such an anointing that words tumbled forth as I spoke in a loud voice—as if preaching. The words came so fast they seemed dictated.

I've never had another experience like that, but I know how a minister feels when he's anointed to preach. I know how the Psalmist felt when he said,

"Thou anointest my head with oil; my cup runneth over" (Psalm 23:5). I've never been a shouter or noisemaker in church, but that occasion was special.

That new touch of the Holy Spirit changed my life. I found that Thompson, Utah fulfilled the desires of my heart. I prayed that God would send me a helper to start a Sunday school in Thompson. Within a week a Baptist lady, Doris Louton, moved to town and we became acquainted and began making plans.

Doris and I had the privilege of telling the story of Jesus to many children who had never heard the name of God or Jesus except as a curse word. We got permission to have the Sunday school in the schoolhouse and, in a short time, we had every child in town enrolled—including some eighth graders who we sometimes took to Moab with us on Sunday nights.

The townspeople were grateful and proud of what we were doing. The two women who had wanted me to play for the tap dancers became my best supporters. One of them told me how much my lessons had made an impression on her 5-year-old son, Dennis.

The previous week I'd given an object lesson of how Jesus Christ can make a black, sinful heart clean and white as snow. The mother had found some "artwork" that had been done with a crayon on her refrigerator a few days later.

"Did you do that?" she asked Dennis.

"No," he said, trying to look innocent.

A little later he ran up to her and fell into her arms, crying. "I did color on the 'frigerator, Mom!" he sobbed. "I don't want my heart to be all black!"

One child was tremendously upset when we told the story of the Crucifixion the Sunday before Easter.

"They killed Him," he muttered, his lower lip protruding and tears filling his eyes.

Since they had never heard it before, I gave them a preview of the Easter lesson. And oh, the joy of telling them that Jesus Christ not only came out of the grave but is alive today! (Incidentally, several parents attended Easter Sunday and listened to our choruses and my flannelgraph-story presentation.)

Because of my bold profession of Christianity, my life was watched by the people of Thompson. To my dismay, however, I became involved in a ring of gossip that traveled throughout the town and back to the lady who was the subject of it.

The lady, who had no children, had brought beer for the adults who attended a child's birthday party. Later that day in the grocery store, the proprietor said, "What did you think of the birthday party?"

I had presumed I was the only one who refused beer, so I said, "What do you mean?"

"I mean what did you think of the beer?" she asked bluntly.

"I was sure surprised to see beer at a child's birthday party," I admitted.

The lady in the grocery store had a Mormon background, and I was delighted to know that she also thought the beer had been out of place. Since I'd started the Sunday school, she had moved the grocery store her husband owned into her home—out of the bar. She'd bought her four children a set of Bible storybooks and was having family devotions with them. I was thrilled with what was happening in her life.

A few days after the birthday party, someone came to me and asked if I'd started the criticism about the woman who'd brought the beer. The object of the gossip was deeply offended and said she'd never again attend one of Thompson's social functions. Her deep hurt made quite a few citizens mad, and since I was the religious teetotaler in town, they deducted that I must have started the gossip.

God told me the incident would hurt my Sunday school if I didn't do something. I prayed and shed a lot of tears, but God told me to go to the woman who had been offended.

As I walked up the gravel road to her mobile home, I kept thinking it was stupid to go. Yet, I was compelled. When they opened the trailer door for me, a look of both shock and disgust crossed the faces of the woman and her husband.

"May I come in?" I asked.

I was shaking so I started slowly. "I've heard about you being hurt by gossip," I began. "I'm sorry. I didn't start the gossip, but I participated in it. I'm fully aware that gossip is as great or greater a sin than drinking—or anything else for that matter—and I want to apologize."

I cried and they cried. I felt love for them and felt they loved me in return. Later, one of their neighbors told me they said I was the first *real* Christian they had seen in their lives and the couple must have been in their late fifties!

God used Thompson to bring spiritual growth and fruit into my life. Because I had so much time to do things, I became interested in Christian writing and journalism. My ministry, which had always been confined to a small group in a church, was expanded through writing—by which I could minister to half a million people with one story or article!

It was a miracle of God when I got a job as a staff reporter in Pueblo, Colorado less than a week after moving there. I'd had brief journalism experience as a newspaper correspondent in Thompson and I had worked several months as a reporter for a small newspaper in Leadville, Colorado. Pueblo, however, is a city of 100,000 and I had had no college or even journalism training in high school.

In a short time after joining the Pueblo staff, I was in charge of the church page and some of my stories were like putting a tract on every doorstep in town. God led me into a tremendous ministry.

I've shared these experiences to show that the Holy Spirit can and will use a dedicated life. I could easily have missed a fantastic blessing and experience if I hadn't taken my cup back for another "running-over" filling. Many times Satan was ready to devour my life and testimony. I'm glad I resisted him and submitted to God.

I hope I haven't led you to believe that the Holy Spirit has made me superior to other Christians. The Baptism doesn't necessarily make me better than other Christians, but it sure makes me better than I'd be without the infilling of power!

As I've told others, there is nothing a person can do, have, or be that compares to the joy that comes with receiving and obeying the Holy Spirit. My wedding day, our first new car, my first by-line on the front page of a newspaper—none compares with the joy Jesus gives.

Despite all this, a peace treaty hasn't been signed with Satan yet, for when I think the battle with that sneaky fellow has been won, he thinks up new strategy.

3

Marked With Red

I've always said God put red hair on some people for the same reason He placed a red spot on the black widow spider. It means danger!

I'm a freckled-faced redhead, so I should know. My flaming hair was always a terrific excuse for my short temper. At least, I used this excuse with other people. Somehow, it never did satisfy my own conscience.

It was my temper that Satan used to try to quench my testimony. I didn't get riled at friends or neighbors, but at home anger sometimes consumed me.

Although I'd had periods of temper fits when my mother-in-law used to live with us for 8 months at a time (I didn't say anything, but did I burn!), and I'd occasionally scream at our first two children, it wasn't until 6 years after our second child's birth when we began to add to our family that I discovered my temper was such a problem.

Fiction writers say that true character is revealed during periods of stress. After the fourth child, and 3 years later the fifth child, came my life was filled with stress. And I didn't like what that stress revealed in me.

One day after witnessing to a neighbor I felt condemned. True, I'd helped her. One of her friends had come from another state for tests on her little boy's heart in a Denver hospital. A blood clot had developed in the boy's arm after the test and the doctors said if the clot didn't dissolve in a few hours it would probably move to the heart and kill the child. They were considering taking the clot out, which may have left the child's arm useless.

The boy's mother was staying with my neighbor, but was at the hospital when I went next door to pick up some Avon cosmetics. The neighbor tearfully told me her friend's trouble. I talked to her at length about divine healing, explaining the miracles I'd seen. I went home, marked Psalm 91 for them, then took the Bible and asked her to give it to her friend when she returned from the hospital.

Her friend wept as she read the promises God had given the Psalmist and claimed them for her son. The next morning doctors encircled the boy's bed, trying to decide what to do. Then they discovered the clot was gone!

The mother knew God had intervened and my neighbor was faithful in thanking me for caring and helping them pray. Nevertheless, my neighbor didn't act interested in God and she never attended church. I was going to witness to her again when suddenly I was almost ashamed at the thought of *me* telling *her* she needed to get saved.

Aren't Christians supposed to be more holy than their unsaved neighbors? I realized that I had never once heard my calm brunette neighbor yell at her son, an only child. She was always doing things for others.

I knew she'd heard my voice shouting in anger at my children more than once. She probably was a better person than me. Yet, I reasoned, give her five children—with one of them needing something while the others are busy writing on freshly painted walls, scratching the furniture, spilling milk, or fighting—maybe then she wouldn't be so calm.

My conscience was clear as far as worldly indulgences were concerned. Yet when I read in 1 Corinthians 13:5 that love (the most important ingredient in a Christian's life) "is not easily provoked," I began to wonder about myself.

Then I read Henry Drummond's book *The Greatest Thing in the World.* He says: "No form of vice—not worldliness, not greed of gold, not drunkenness itself—does more to unChristianize society than evil temper. For embittering life, for breaking up communities, for destroying the most sacred relationships, for devastating homes, for withering up men and women, for taking the bloom of childhood; in short, for sheer gratuitous, misery-producing power, this influence stands alone" (Old Tappan, NJ: Fleming H. Revell Co., 1968, p. 35).

Now that got to my conscience.

Biblical prophecy was being fulfilled on every hand and I knew that the Lord Jesus Christ might return at any moment (1 Thessalonians 4:16, 17). I began to wonder if I was ready to meet Him.

Sometimes when I went to bed at night I nearly panicked, fearing the Lord would come before morning. I'd remember the anger I'd displayed that day— yelling like crazy when I'd found that the kids had spilled glue all over the cedar closet floor and then thrown newspapers on top of it; or how angry I was when I had come home from the grocery store and the assigned work still wasn't done.

I remember wondering how I could ever have felt worthy to share my testimony. I wasn't better than my unsaved neighbors and I knew it.

One night as I lay awake wondering if I could possibly get to heaven, God revealed the answer to me: No! I wasn't good enough in myself. That was the reason I needed a Saviour. That was why God had sent His Son. His righteousness makes me righteous. When I have Christ's blood applied to my heart, God sees Christ's righteousness: "For he hath made him to be sin for us, who knew no sin; that we might be made the righteousness of God in him" (2 Corinthians 5:21).

Then I remembered that God doesn't like our own righteousness anyhow: "But we are all as an unclean thing, and all our righteousnesses are as filthy rags" (Isaiah 64:6).

While my neighbor appeared to be good, she couldn't make heaven without Christ's atonement. So despite my failures, I had to continue to witness to her, while I asked God to help me with my temper. (It has been so much easier to control since I realized I don't have to do it all by myself.)

Some good, moral people ignore God, yet think that when the end comes, because they are good, they will be given a passport to heaven. But ignoring God is one of the gravest sins, for Christ said we should "love the Lord [our] God with all [our] heart, and with all [our] soul, and with all [our] mind, and with all [our] strength" (Mark 12:30). When a person goes his own way without God, he is committing sin.

"Good" people also need a Saviour. This time the mark of red (in contrast to the black widow) doesn't mean danger, it means safety—for through the red blood shed by our Lord on Calvary we can obtain His righteousness. "All we like sheep have gone astray; we have turned every one to his own way; and the Lord hath laid on him the iniquity of us all" (Isaiah 53:6).

I discovered His blood is powerful enough to cover the sins of anyone—even a redhead—and once again I began to bring my light out where it could shine. In fact, I nearly worked myself to death trying to light the whole world with my candle.

Would you believe the enemy even found a way to try to destroy me through my church work?

4

A Flickering Flame

It was in the supermarket, while I was wondering whether or not to indulge in a pound of bacon, that it happened. My emotions knotted inside me as a trumpet blasted. The knot exploded into currents of joy that flowed through every molecule of me.

Jesus! Oh, Jesus! my soul rejoiced. The greatest thrill I'd ever felt filled me as gravity no longer held my feet but pulled me from above and I began to rise. As if from a great compulsion, others were being lifted in a mass exodus from the earth.

Oh, Lord Jesus, You've come! You've come!

The wonder and satisfaction I felt filled me long after I'd awakened and discovered it was a dream. But I knew someday it will be reality.

For much of my life, I began each day thinking, "Lord, will you come today?" and each night trying to make sure I had everything right with God before going to sleep.

The Church has been excited about the nearness of Christ's coming throughout my lifetime. As Jews began returning to Palestine and Israel finally became a nation, we knew it was the fulfillment of Ezekiel 37. The dry bones of the Jewish nation, scattered all over the world, had "connected." God indeed had caused the nation of Israel to "live again." He breathed life into them and placed them in their own land, which was a sign that the time of the Gentiles had nearly been fulfilled and the rapture of the Church was at hand.[1]

That was one reason I believed in working for the Lord. It seemed there was not much time left.

When we moved to Denver, the church we chose was small, but filled with dedicated young couples. Almost unanimously the congregation attended that church because we believed in the old-fashioned gospel the pastor preached—total commitment to God. All the young couples desired to serve God totally. When we visited in each others' homes, we usually got around to talking about the Lord. We were full of the fire of the Holy Ghost and ready to do exploits for God.

We worked together, prayed together, wept together, and laughed together. We witnessed, visited homes of the unsaved, and brought sinners to church with us. We prayed and worked around the altar. We taught Sunday school classes and worked with teenagers. We had missionary projects for both home and foreign missions.

We had special prayer meetings. We sang together and we shared burdens. We cleaned the church and the church yard and planted plants and shrubs. We had bake sales to buy carpeting for the sanctuary and made draperies and decorated the Sunday school rooms.

A whole nucleus of people (a majority of the congregation) was involved in the Lord's work. We had few "pew performers" who only kept 18 inches of a pew warm once a week. We were at the church usually four or five times a week—and sometimes more.

At this time, I thought it was my responsibility to be at the church every time the door was open for any purpose. (Most pastors today *value* those kind of members.) For me, however, I got so involved with teaching a high school class, visitation, prayer meetings, playing the piano for three services a week (and sometimes choir practice), that I began to have trouble with my nerves. I believed (and still do) that anyone who neglects his own home is worse than an infidel, so I was also trying to keep things perfect at home—a clean house and well-prepared meals—and give my family plenty of attention. I continued to write and had about 10 piano students I was teaching "evangelistic piano."

I had the idea that if I hurried fast enough, I could do all the things I wanted to do, as well as the things I felt obligated to do.

Suddenly, my world dominoed. First, my nerves became so edgy that the slightest thing that happened at home appeared to be a near disaster and I could get into a state of panic over almost nothing. I began having muscle spasms which could only be relieved by medication.

It dawned on me that I was tired, tired, tired, and on the verge of a nervous breakdown. I prayed for release from my nervous problem, but instead of victory I kept thinking about harming the temple of God, and I realized that by overworking I had brought on the condition in which I found myself.

I began giving up responsibilities. I resigned my class. I asked the pastor to use other pianists. I quit attending any church functions except the Sunday and Wednesday services.

As I stepped out of my leadership roles, I replaced responsibilities with hostilities. I had more time to notice the appearance of others. I'd always hated being a freckled-faced redhead, and as I watched the attractive, well-dressed women of the church, I began to resent the money they had for beauty products, clothing, and accessories. Many of them sewed, but as elaborate as their wardrobes were, I knew even at $5 a dress they were spending far more money than I could. Although I still loved them, I inwardly winced at their beauty, their fancy new outfits, and their wigs and hairpieces.

My husband got a second job so I learned to sew and spent much of my time mentally designing outfits. Les gave me a wig that exactly matched my hair color but was much prettier and easier to style than my own heavy natural curl.

During this time I desired, as always, to see souls saved. It seemed, however, that when I stopped working in the church so did everyone else. (This was a lie from Satan, the father of lies, because the church continued to survive.) I watched sinners come and go to our services without making a commitment. It seemed our altars were always empty. We had to dismiss at noon on Sunday morning no matter what. (I thought the pastor and the rest of the men were in a hurry to get home to watch football.)

The pastor usually gave an invitation to sinners, but rarely did anyone respond. Christians, however, almost *never* were asked to pray in a general altar call, and I thought the sinners probably felt we were more interested in going home than in praying someone through to a personal relationship with Jesus and eternal life. I thought if the Christians would go forward on Sunday morning—at least part of the time—sinners would not feel they were infringing on our time but only joining us in something we wanted to do.

I felt we'd become little more than a club. I was critical of each service. The microphones were too loud. We weren't organized anymore. Satan told me we were getting absolutely nothing done. I was more discouraged after going to church than I had been before I went.

My discouragement went even further. I quit writing because I had nothing to say. I began focusing my total attention on me, my problems, and the faults of others. I found myself with a severe case of the "pride of life" (1 John 2:16) while I sat in the "seat of the scornful" (Psalm 1:1), worrying about every trivial thing that came into my life.

I'd forgotten that Jesus could come any day and He'd judge me for *my* deeds, not the works of others. When I heard a sermon on the Rapture or Second Coming, I'd think, *Oh yes, He is coming back!* But there was no joyful expectancy anymore. If Jesus had come then like a thief in the night (as He said He would) I don't know if I'd have felt that change in the pull of gravity or heard the trumpet.

If I had missed the Rapture, it wouldn't have been because I'd given up my responsibilities—I had had to.

It wouldn't have been because I had decided to pay more attention to personal beauty and concentrate on being more attractive.

It wouldn't have been only because I was caught in a snare of criticism.

It wouldn't have been because I was discouraged.

It would have been because I had taken my eyes off Jesus—the "author and finisher of our faith" (Hebrews 12:2). If I had kept my eyes on Jesus, I would have known He could keep a church going without *my* help (it was a very humbling experience when this finally dawned on me). If I had kept my eyes on Jesus, I wouldn't have allowed the pride of life to take a top position in my priorities. If I had kept my eyes on Jesus, I wouldn't have had time to feel sorry for myself.

If I had only looked at Jesus—the Prince of Peace; our Saviour, Healer, and Baptizer; the Beginning and the End; the Lily of the Valley; the Bright and Morning Star; our soon-coming King.

To be ready for the Rapture of the Church, I believe Jesus must have *first* place in our lives—not fourth, third, or even second—but *number one!* God is a jealous God (Exodus 20:5) and unto those that look for Him shall He appear the second time (Hebrews 9:28).

I couldn't see Jesus, however, because I was looking at my own problems. Instead of circumstances getting better, they got worse. But, thank God, my nervous condition began to improve just at the time I was facing another crisis. Craig, our fourth child, developed chronic bronchial asthma and the disease became so severe I began to live a nightmare.

---

[1]The Rapture of the Church is the saints "meeting" the Lord in the air to go to the Marriage Supper of the Lamb while the earth is engaged in the Great Tribulation and the Battle of Armageddon. The Second Coming is when Jesus comes *to* earth, His feet touching the Mount of Olives, and He brings the saints with Him to judge the world. (See 1 Thessalonians 4:13-17; Luke 17:34-36; Zechariah 14:4.)

5

Entering the
Troubled Waters

I bent over my child's crib, watching his breathing. Yes, he was having difficulty again. The wheezing was gaining momentum.

Panic seized me. I shut the bedroom door to shield me from the sounds of my husband and other children. We'd prayed together for Craig on other occasions, but now I wanted to be alone. Craig, only 2, had been hospitalized several times for acute bronchial asthma. At first, shots of adrenaline or a night or two in a "croup tent" had brought relief. But the asthma attacks became more serious and frequent. I was horrified by the possible side effects of the medicines he was required to take. Then the doctor said I had to give him shots of adrenaline at home myself when he had an attack. I thought I couldn't do it, but somehow I learned how, avoiding the pleading, tortured expression in his eyes, and got the job done.

But that wasn't the end of the nightmare. One night, after giving him a shot, he continued to wheeze loudly. His stomach pumped convulsively trying to force air through his lungs.

The doctor on call wasn't aware of the gravity of Craig's asthma and told me to administer another shot (although it wasn't time for another one yet) and said Craig would be all right.

Craig continued to wheeze the rest of the night and gained no relief, even with the vaporizer going full blast, steam treatments, alternated with a whiff of cold air (which I'd been informed should help, and sometimes did), and all the medication I dared give him.

I reached the regular doctor about 7 a.m. and he told me to go straight to the hospital. An intravenous tube was inserted into Craig's tiny arm and he was admitted to the pediatric ward. But instead of getting better, his breathing got worse. I'd been praying constantly and continued to do so as I ran and told a nurse he was getting worse. The doctor came, even though it was during office hours. I rushed to a phone and called everyone I could think of to pray.

Finally it seemed Craig couldn't get another breath. "Mama!" he cried as he gasped hysterically for air, his arms outstretched to me as he peered through the plastic tent. "Mama!"

Steroid drugs (of the cortisone family) were inserted into the intravenous tube and mainlined into Craig's bloodstream. The doctor and nurses looked at me to see how I was taking it as Craig struggled to breathe. I kept praying. They let me stay.

It was about an hour before relief came. Later a nurse commented, "Your little boy sure came out of it fast. If they come out of it, they usually do snap back fast."

I praised God every time I watched him breathe. But temporary relief wasn't all I wanted. I knew God was able to heal him completely.

But more asthma attacks came. More hospitalizations. More prayer. And always steroids. Often when Craig was released from the hospital his body was swollen and puffy from the side effects of the strong drugs. Hospital personnel always had trouble finding a vein for the intravenous tube. He underwent agony not only with the asthma, but also with the treatment.

He couldn't sleep through the night. Often I'd be up with him a dozen times or more, giving him medicine, filling the vaporizer, trying respiratory therapy (hand clapping on the chest, sides, and back), and often just to check on him.

I learned that once steroids are begun in an asthmatic patient, it is difficult to get by without using a form of cortisone for any kind of illness. It was almost certain that when he had an attack, or even a cold, he'd have to have steroids unless he could go at least 6 months without getting sick.

I discovered that many asthmatics have serious side effects from the steroids—ulcers, stunted growth, softened bones, water retention in tissues. Not only does the drug cause problems, but also higher and higher dosages probably would be required as Craig grew older—and the drug might eventually lose its effectiveness.

The day I shut the bedroom door to pray for Craig, I had just gotten him out of the hospital. As he began to convulsively wheeze again, I felt as if I had gone as far as I could go. As soon as I shut the door, I broke into hysterical sobs.

"God!" I cried. "Lord Jesus!"

I began to evaluate my belief in divine healing. I acknowledged that persons who seemed more worthy than I had not received desired miracles. Several pastors and missionaries of my acquaintance had been stricken with cancer and not healed.

Who am I to expect a miracle when these are not raised up? I thought.

My mind went through the basics of my beliefs. Did I really believe in God? *Yes!* I immediately answered. The awe-inspiring creation of God couldn't have happened without a Creator.

Did I believe in salvation? *Yes!* I had seen changed lives and had interviewed many who were saved from a life of sin and had experienced real joy for the first time after being born again. Although I was saved as a child, I knew the satisfaction of knowing Jesus as my personal Saviour.

Then I remembered that healing for the body was purchased at the same time as redemption for the soul. I looked up some Scripture passages:

> . . . He hath sent me to heal the brokenhearted, to preach deliverance to the captives, and *recovering of sight to the blind, to set at liberty them that are bruised* (Luke 4:18).

> But he was wounded for our transgressions, he was bruised for our iniquities: the chastisement of our peace was upon him; and *with his stripes we are healed* (Isaiah 53:5).

I recalled the miracles I had observed during my life as a Pentecostal. There was my chum, Velda Jean Bailey, who was stricken with leukemia and the disease was in the last stages before it was discovered. I was probably about 13 or 14 and she was a year or two younger than me, but we had played together in her home on several occasions.

My brother-in-law told me about her condition.

"The doctors say Velda Jean probably has only 2 or 3 weeks to live."

Then a woman in the Fruita church tearfully requested prayer for Velda during a Sunday morning service. "Velda's parents didn't realize she was listening when they received the report from the doctor. The child began screaming, 'I don't want to die! I don't want to die!' "

The episode struck terror to my heart. I thought of Velda Jean day and night and the thought that something similar could happen to me or someone in my family caused me to live on the edge of panic.

Then the joyous news came! Velda Jean and her grandfather had been praying together in the bedroom. Her knees had been so tender and swollen that not even a bed sheet could touch them without her crying.

When her grandfather brought her out of the bedroom and laid her on the couch, her mother saw a change coming over her daughter as if new blood was going into her veins. Her symptoms disappeared. Her parents asked for new tests. The doctors found that Velda Jean Bailey was completely healed, and she is alive at this writing—25 years later!

I had seen and heard of many other miracles. Sure, I'd read articles that said healing evangelists were fakes and used actors who threw away their crutches during services. In nearly every church I attended, however, there were scores of people with testimonies of miraculous answers to prayer.

In Lakewood, Colorado, where we attended church for nearly 8 years, a deacon twisted his ankle and tore ligaments. Doctors X-rayed and wrapped his ankle and told him to rent crutches and not work for a few days. The deacon (Gary Hilgers) called the pastor. When the pastor prayed, the swelling went down immediately and the bandage dangled loosely. Only 2 or 3 hours after telling his boss he'd be off work for several days, Gary walked into the office without a limp and told them what had happened.

Our friends, Mark and Joy Wood, whose daughter was born a hydrocephalic (water on the brain), have kept in touch with us throughout the past 23 years. When Becky was born to them, her head began to enlarge and the diagnosis was made. X rays and treatments showed there was no hope for her recovery and she would be hopelessly retarded. Because of the other children in the home, doctors recommended she be placed in an institution.

Before sending the baby to the State Home for the Retarded in Grand Junction, Mark and Joy called their pastor, Rev. Kenneth Schmidt. He anointed the child with oil, put his hands on her enlarged skull, and prayed.

In only a matter of weeks, the baby's body and head were proportionately correct and she recognized her mother. After careful observation she was declared completely normal and sent home to her parents. Becky is now a healthy, vibrant teenager who has dedicated her life to God. She joyfully shares her testimony with others.

There was also the Owens boy who was healed of sugar diabetes as a young child. Before moving to Florence, Colorado his parents attended the church in Fruita. When their child was diagnosed as having chronic childhood diabetes, their daughter, Mrs. Juanita Ward, requested prayer for her brother in the Fruita church and in several neighboring churches.

After several weeks of diligent prayer, the boy was retested and found free of the disease. He never had another recurrence and today is married and living in the Denver area.

There had been numerous less dramatic healings. And in my child's room that night during hours of agonizing prayer I recalled many: Marjorie Eager, whose blood clot vanished instantly after she'd suffered for 6 weeks with it; Kim Butrick who was healed of a heart murmur; the Combs girl in Pueblo whose serious heart ailment was healed and the entire family was saved as a result (even aunts and uncles).

Finally I said, "God, I don't know why some are healed and some are not, but I am convinced that You not only came to save the soul, but to heal the body. Your Word declares it. There is evidence to prove You have performed the miraculous. Whether or not you see fit to heal Craig, I will believe in divine healing."

The answer to Craig's problem hasn't come the way I had hoped. He didn't have to go back to the hospital that night, but in later months his condition deteriorated until he was completely covered with eczema and was having asthma attacks so frequently that all the nurses in the pediatrics ward of the large Denver hospital where we took him knew him by name.

The pediatrician did allergy tests, but he didn't believe the results were significant. We took him to a chiropractor several times a week, but still no dramatic results. We continued to seek God. Finally the pediatrician suggested putting him on small dosages of prednisone every other day, even when he was well. I knew this would probably bring temporary relief from the asthma and eczema but it would be the beginning of a downhill fight with steroids.

In desperation, I called my Catholic charismatic neighbor and asked the name of her allergist. I made an appointment.

The results were shocking. Craig could eat no wheat, eggs, milk or milk products, chocolate, fish, corn, tomatoes, or citrus products, and beef only on special occasions. I thought it was going to be impossible to prepare meals without the forbidden items, but it was possible. Dramatic relief from the eczema came immediately. For the asthma (in addition to the diet), strict procedures had to be taken to desensitize his room and he had to be given regular desensitizing injections for molds, dusts, and pollens.

His need for medication immediately dropped. He began sleeping all night. Attacks have become less frequent and less severe. He has been off the cortisone for nearly 3 years. He can tolerate small amounts of substances (including foods) to which he'd been allergic. The healing is gradual, and I thank God.

Perhaps God wants me to use "faith and works" with Craig for a gradual healing. (Some children "grow out" of asthma, but doctors gave me little hope of this.) I'd like to see a complete miracle for Craig. While he's small (9 years old) I feel my faith is vital to victory.

In the past 2 or 3 years, God has performed miracles in our home. Our daughter Gwen had a hearing deficiency and tests revealed she had fluid in the inner ear and needed surgery to insert tubes to drain the fluid.

We took Gwen for prayer several times but the condition only worsened. One Sunday night as a Spirit-filled layman placed his hands on her and prayed, she said her ears tickled. The tests that had been scheduled for the preoperation exam showed the fluid was gone and her hearing was perfect!

Then the baby, Jeanette, dislocated her elbow as she pulled back and someone else pulled on her hand. The doctor put the bones back in place and said the joint was underdeveloped. The episode was extremely painful to Jeanette. In fact, she couldn't use her arm as long as the bones were dislocated.

Only a few days after the doctor had put it back in place, she dislocated it again. This time he told me to put it back in place myself, while he directed me over the phone. When I tried to put it back in place she screamed. So I stopped, prayed awhile, and tried again. Finally, I got it replaced.

When it dislocated the third time, I called the doctor and he said to keep trying to get the joint in place myself because the delay caused by traveling to his office would make the joint even more difficult to connect correctly.

"Since the joint has become dislocated three times," the pediatrician said when I took Jeanette for a checkup, "you'd better take her to an orthopedic specialist." He scrawled a name on a pad. "The arm could become permanently useless unless something is done. The orthopedist probably will put the arm in a cast for several months."

When I walked back to the car after hearing his advice, I realized I hadn't had Jeanette prayed for. The next Sunday night we took her for prayer and the arm never became dislocated again, even though the other kids kept forgetting and pulling on it.

My uncle, Wilford Shepherd, went totally blind when his eyes hemorrhaged a few weeks after a cataract operation. Eye surgeons gave little hope he would ever see again.

"You might try prayer," one Pueblo, Colorado doctor suggested.

People all over the United States were praying. I requested prayer at our church.

One day after coming to Denver for a checkup with a famous eye specialist, he called me.

"I can see the outline of my coffee cup," he said, his voice choking up.

Not many months later, he got his driver's license back. Uncle Willie is now about 70 years old and the doctors say his sight is a miracle.

Then only about a year ago, my niece who lives in Colorado Springs had a baby whom doctors said was born with a heart defect. Only a few days after his birth, plans were being made to rush him to Children's Hospital in Denver. After much prayer and God's intervention, instead of going to Denver the baby went home with his mother in good health.

God is so good!

6

Grave Clothes of Discouragement

In addition to physical healing, I've found the Lord gives emotional healing.

When I think of how He instantly healed me after a long period of discouragement, I am reminded of a story my mother-in-law told me:

During the Great Depression, a young woman stopped at an Oklahoma farmhouse and asked for water. In the farmhouse, a teenager was mixing chocolate and sugar in a bowl to add to a recipe.

Suddenly the visitor grabbed the bowl from the teenaged girl and licked up all the chocolate mixture. As she finished, the stranger looked into the eyes of the startled young cook. The woman blinked and hung her head.

"I'm so ashamed," she confessed. "I shouldn't have done that, but I was so hungry—and the chocolate looked so good, I couldn't control myself!"

The depression of the 1930s caused many to suffer hunger. While I've never experienced the hardships of intense physical hunger, I've gone through periods of discouragement that made me think there was a spiritual famine. Sometimes I almost wished I could reach out and take some of the blessings others were receiving when my soul felt empty and on the verge of spiritual starvation.

During the time Craig required so much hospitalization and care, I was emotionally and physically drained. Although it shouldn't have, this affected my spiritual life—like a worm eating away the fruit of the Spirit in my life. Joy and peace seemed to shrivel and die inside of me, and discouragement took their place. In addition, I became pregnant again, and 3 months after Jeanette (the fifth child) was born, I had to have major surgery.

Jeanette was only about 6 months old when we found Craig was allergic to mold in the basement of the church we attended. The basement had flooded several times, and the carpeting and even the walls were full of mold. The doctor said the mold could filter up into the sanctuary and we noticed Craig often began getting ill at church. One night after he had broken out in hives and had an asthma attack during a service, we knew we had to change churches. In fact, the doctor insisted on it.

For several months we looked for a place to worship. We attended many fine Pentecostal churches. In spite of my season of criticism, I missed my former pastor, his wife, and my friends. I felt no one could preach as well as my former pastor. I loved and admired his wife. I missed my friends; they were almost as close to me as family.

I also missed feeling I belonged to a church. Even after visiting the same church several times in a row, I felt uncomfortable and as if I didn't belong.

My lack of joy must have showed at home. I wasn't aware that I frowned most of the time until Craig was looking at one of the little "people" that came with a pull toy. One of the little wooden boys had a terrible frown.

"That's you, Mommy," he told me.

To remind myself to smile and look pleasant, I tried putting smiley faces around the house and looking in the mirror each time I passed, but my face refused to show something I didn't feel inside.

Finally we decided to regularly attend the church nearest our home. One night as the congregation was standing around the altar praising the Lord, I watched a young woman who was receiving a blessing. The church (which we now love) was composed mainly of new Christians and recently Spirit-filled members from other denominations. I thought she probably was a new convert.

As she stood with her face beaming and tears dripping off her cheeks, reveling in the joy of the Lord, I grinned almost jealously and said, "Lord, couldn't you give me a little blessing just because of my seniority?"

I felt like the tigers at the zoo look at feeding time, saliva dripping from their jaws, as they pace back and forth waiting for food. My innermost being cried out for spiritual nourishment. Yet, as I prayed and went through the forms of worship, it was tasteless to my soul. The river of joy in my soul was dried up. I couldn't cry. I couldn't rejoice. I could praise with my mouth, but it wasn't coming from my soul. It seemed I was bound with something I couldn't shake loose.

One Sunday night several months after we had begun attending the church, our pastor asked those who needed a touch from God to stand. I stood. I felt no emotion as he prayed, then slowly peace filled my soul. When the congregation began singing some choruses, it was as if the grave clothes of discouragement that had bound me had dropped away. The presence of the Lord felt so refreshing! The service was over, but people were sitting around singing. We sang choruses. We sang songs from the book. I sat down and enjoyed it.

A trickle in the river of joy had begun to dribble in my soul. Gradually it increased until it was tumbling through again, and although that was about 5 years ago, it's still flowing. Some days the river seems to be trying to overflow its banks, while on others there are only a few ripples flowing—yet the drought is past.

There are many other spiritual experiences and lessons the Lord has brought into my life. I hope I am learning what He wishes to teach me. In the following chapters I will share some of these experiences and lessons.

7

Thanks

A few years ago I spent a winter in 2-mile-high Leadville, Colorado, the city that is so cold during the winter that silver kings in the early part of this century spent $100,000 to build an ice palace there—and their investment lasted several months!

Leadville was still cold when we moved there, but the severity of the winters didn't make an impact on me until one night in January. Les, my husband, was working in another town. He'd left me strict instructions to keep the bathtub water faucet running a little because the electric heat tape he'd put on the pipes under our mobile home wasn't long enough to cover them.

Other evenings I had faithfully followed his instructions, but that cold January night I took a bath and forgot to turn the water back on. Four hours later my mother-in-law got out of bed and turned on the water. A sucking sound beneath the floor made the mobile home shudder. I awoke and instantly knew the pipes were frozen.

I jumped out of bed, put a big coat on over my nightclothes, grabbed a fuse torch, and went out into the cold. I knew if I waited until morning the pipes would be broken.

After making a tunnel through the deep snow with a broom, I crawled to the water pipes. Already I was freezing. I tried to light the torch, but my matches wouldn't light. I had gotten them wet in the snow.

Hurriedly I crawled back out of the tunnel and dashed for the trailer door. My bare hand stuck to the frosty doorknob. The door wouldn't open! I pulled but nothing happened. The warmth from the mobile home had caused some of the deep snow on the roof to melt, run down, and then freeze on the metal sides. The door had frozen shut!

I pulled and pulled. I was so cold, I was hurting. (Now I know why they call it frost*bite*.) I began praying I would get back inside. I knew none of the neighbors and I was ashamed to go to them at 2 a.m. the way I was dressed and confess my stupidity. I prayed some more.

Finally I rang the doorbell. My mother-in-law was asleep. She had been able to get enough water so she didn't realize the pipes were frozen. I didn't want to tell her what I'd done, but now I had to. I began yelling and I kept ringing the bell. At last she came and I shouted my problem to her. She pushed on the door (although she wasn't very strong) and I pulled.

I prayed some more. After what seemed like a decade, the ice cracked and the door swung open. Shivering and feeling frozen stiff, I stepped into the warmth inside.

When I prepared to go back outside, I dressed for the occasion. I put on several layers of warm clothing, boots, a coat, a hat, and gloves. I left the door open a little and made sure my matches stayed out of the snow. Soon the pipes were thawed and I was snuggled back in bed again.

I praised God for the warmth and protection from the cold. I praised Him for the dripping faucet I could hear in the bathroom. I praised Him that I had gotten back inside before I suffered frostbite. I thanked God the pipes weren't broken. I even praised Him for my mother-in-law!

I didn't praise the Lord, however, that I had been stupid enough to turn off the water and not turn it back on. I didn't praise Him for the short electric tape that had caused the problem. I didn't praise Him for the 32-degree-below-zero weather outside either.

It never occurred to me to praise Him for the bad things that crossed my path. I usually looked for, and found, something good for which I could praise the Lord about in every major event in my life.

In recent years, it has become widely preached that the Christian should praise God not *in* all things, but *for* all things—including the big disasters and the small annoyances and frustrations of life.

It's not proper, I told myself, *to praise God for illness, disaster, heartache, and trouble.* (In the first place, God didn't send it, although He *allows* it.)

I still agree with this philosophy in part. There is always something good for which we can thank God. This isn't just beneficial for getting the answer to the problem at hand. Counting our blessings is good mental therapy. If we obey Philippians 4:8 and think of the just, pure, holy, lovely, and good things, the peace of God will keep our hearts and minds. We can bring ourselves from the pit of despair to the peak of contentment through praise.

Yet, I have heard testimonies and seen people who found victory only when they praised God *for* an almost intolerable situation.

In our church I heard the story of a young lady who had been injured in a car accident. For 7 years she was hospitalized in a mental institution because the injury had caused brain damage.

The young woman's father, a Christian, prayed for his daughter often. Yet, he couldn't help feeling a little bitter about what God had allowed to happen to his beautiful girl.

One day as the father was driving on a busy street, God said, "Praise Me for your daughter's condition."

"No, God. I can't," he argued.

"Praise Me," God still impressed on the man.

Finally, halting words of praise began, "Jesus . . . thank You. . . ."

A few hours later when the father entered the mental hospital to visit his daughter, the young lady ran to him saying, "Daddy! Daddy!" It was the first time she'd recognized him since the accident.

Soon she was released from the hospital, mentally competent. Hospital personnel and the young lady said her mind was restored at the same moment the father began praising God for her hopeless condition.

When I heard the story, I didn't know what to think about it. I couldn't forget it. . . . finally I asked God to teach me about praise. It was less than a week later when God began showing me where I needed to praise Him. Somehow, I'd always believed the big things in life were totally controlled by God and accepted them as His will. But the small things were a different story! I found bitterness in my heart over the small daily frustrations.

"Lord," something deep inside kept crying out, "I'm trying to do Your will. I've dedicated my life to

You. How can You let these things happen to me? Are You noticing what's going on down here?"

Actually, I didn't dare allow my mind to dwell on these things, but in my subconscious they were there.

I discovered that *any time there is bitterness* in my heart, if I can praise God for the circumstances, I am on the road to victory. When I praise Him for the bad things, I can get rid of this bitterness and clear the way for an answer to my prayers.

After I praised Him for them, the things that annoyed me and caused bitterness seemed to disappear. Although the circumstances often remained the same, I was able to rise above them and obtain victory in spite of the previous obstacles.

I remember standing by the sink one day thanking God for one of my problems. Tears were dripping onto the pans I was scrubbing. As my bitterness melted away into genuine praise, my problem melted too. Several months later, I noticed I was *enjoying* the thing that had given me so much grief.

I must say, however, that usually I still find good things for which to praise Him, even when I praise Him for the bad. It is only in special circumstances (when I'm getting bitter or resentful) that I feel I need to do anything other than look for the blessings I can find to thank Him for.

When Paul and Silas sang praises in jail, I don't believe they were bitter at God for their predicament so they didn't need to thank Him that they were in stocks and behind bars. They praised God because of what He had already done and, in faith, because they were confident He was going to bring something good out of their troubles—and He did!

In thanking God for past blessings, I am acknowledging that the Lord was the Source. In praising Him for trials, I am showing that I have faith in Him nevertheless and know all things will work together for good. When I praise Him in advance for my requests I am showing faith.

Best of all, praise can be the faucet that turns on the fountain of joy. I can start whispering, "Precious Jesus . . . sweet Jesus . . . wonderful Saviour. Thank You for Your mercy on me. Thank You for coming so that I can live forever. I love You, Jesus. I praise Your wonderful name."

Then the tears come; my words are no longer adequate. Suddenly it's swelling inside me. Only a heavenly language can express it and it rolls out, uninhibited, praising my Redeemer.

8

The Greening of a Christian

A few years ago residents of a small mountain village were ordered by the city officials to use their private wells for domestic use only. Any watering outside the house was prohibited.

"How can they enforce such a law?" I asked one of my friends who lived there. "Won't there be people who will water their lawns and gardens at night or when they think they won't get caught?"

"Ha!" she laughed. "All the officials have to do is pick out the green grass and flourishing gardens and write out a ticket."

Just as a green lawn shows it has been watered and cared for in midsummer's dry heat, the spiritually "watered" life of the Christian in today's sin-scorched world shows he has tapped "living water."

Contrary to popular belief, a Christian doesn't have to be "trained" to be a witness. The Bible speaks of believers as the "light of the world." When the Holy Spirit sets you on fire others will see your light— unless you hide it.

I haven't always known how simple it is to witness. When I was in my teens and president of the young people's group, one of the first things we had was an emphasis on tract distribution. We ordered a pile of tracts and I tried to inspire the members to start distributing literature. Every Sunday, however, I felt a little weird as we asked for testimonies of results of the tract campaign because, although I'd left tracts in all sorts of places, I hadn't *once* personally handed a tract to someone outside the church.

So I decided to slip somebody a "warm" one. One afternoon as I was walking to town (only two blocks in Fruita) I told the Lord I'd give a tract to the first person I met. Just as I got near the grocery store, the carry-out boy stepped out to sweep the sidewalk. I knew him. He was a senior at my high school. My heart started having convulsions. I took the tract, ran up to the boy, and shoved the paper in his hand.

"Here. Read this!" I choked out. Then I nearly left a patch of shoe sole on the sidewalk as I tried to get away.

A few weeks after my sour experience with handing out tracts, I sat in the study hall around a table with some other students who were discussing the future of the earth in light of wars, the bomb, and so forth. It was easy to speak up and explain Bible prophecy. I could tell no one else there was familiar with God's Word. The group was amazed and interested in what I had to say.

Afterward, I remembered how easily I'd shared the Word, and how my witness had affected the listeners. I discovered that a testimony doesn't have to be worked up. Unless the Christian has let the oil (of the Holy Spirit) in his "lamp" run low, as did the 10 virgins in Matthew 25, or talks himself out of it, witnessing is almost inevitable. This has been true in my life. To my amazement, I've had people ask *me* if they could go to church with me.

When we moved to Denver from Pueblo, a young housewife who lived in the duplex next door continually made a path to my door. I acted around my new friend just as I do around my church friends. We discussed spiritual things, but she didn't want to get too deep. I never gave it a thought when I told her what a great service we had had at church the night before—I was just being myself.

She was continually popping in to ask something, borrow something, or just to chat. She was there so often, I had no chance to make a pretense about what a holy life we live. Day after day she observed us as we were.

"May I go to church with you?" she asked one day. "You enjoy your church and life in general more than anyone I've known."

I was glad to take her with me.

That wasn't the only time someone asked if he could go to church as my guest. When I worked for the newspaper, it was the young girl reporter who sat in front of my desk. In Utah, it was the schoolteacher. There may have been others I've forgotten.

Of course I don't always wait for other people to open the way for me to give a testimony. When I was in the hospital, I was in a room with a young girl who was going to have an abortion. From the instant she arrived in the room I had a compelling urge to witness to her—even before I knew why she was there. I discovered her father was an alcoholic and had disappeared 3 years earlier. Her mother was having men friends come to the house.

Kathy (not her real name) had spent the money she had saved for college on the abortion. She felt she'd come to the end of her road and the future was very dark, even though her boyfriend was still hanging around.

I'd only begun to stay awake for a while after my own surgery when I started talking to her. We had a lot of fun joking around part of the time, then we'd get serious and I'd talk to her about the Lord. Something kept us talking, even when it would have been nice to be quiet and relax.

After the abortion, she cried and then slept a long time. When she began feeling better, we started talking again and I showed her the way of salvation and told her how to pray, but she didn't make a definite decision to follow the Lord.

When she went home, I broke into tears and sobbed uncontrollably.

"She doesn't have a chance in life!" I sobbed to my roommate. "She needs somebody to care what she does!"

Only a few weeks later it was Easter and I received a card from Kathy.

"You'll never know how much I appreciate you," she wrote. I'd given her a book about Eugenia Price's conversion. "Thanks for the book. My life will never be the same."

At Christmas I received another card telling me she would be able to go to college after all and that she and her boyfriend were getting married.

Another time, I began sharing with a young man the trouble I had had when I took an English course and discovered it included study on logic and argumentative persuasion. The young man had majored in logic and debate in college. I mentioned I was a religious writer, and told him how my instructor and I had clashed head-on during the first lesson.

"My instructor said faith has nothing to do with logic," I told the young fellow. "He said I'd better get that understood right away."

"Your teacher's right," the young man said, sitting forward in his chair. "I'm an agnostic. Faith is something a person uses for the unknown—or something of which he's afraid. It's a crutch."

"That's not quite right," I said. "Faith is something everyone uses every day. The atheist has faith in evolution and science—perhaps more faith than many Christians have in God. Some people have faith in education. Everyone lives by faith. Our minds are too small to absorb everything and prove it for ourselves. The doctor has to have faith in the mechanic for his car. When he's ill, the mechanic has to have faith in the doctor."

"I guess that's right," he admitted.

"As far as argumentative persuasion or logic is concerned," I continued, "if someone is going to prove something by argument, the person who is convinced has to have faith in what the individual said who won the argument. If a fact can be proved, there is no need for logic or argument."

As I paused to allow him to express a viewpoint, suddenly I panicked. *Lord, how did I get myself into this? He's a scholar of debate! He's traveled all over the country with debate teams. Help me, Jesus!*

It always seems to help to keep a spirit of mutual respect and love in the conversation when I witness, so I kept using my instructor as an example.

"I told all of this to my instructor," I went on. "I also said, 'You can't prove God doesn't exist and I can't prove that He does. God left this gap that has to be bridged by faith because faith in Jesus Christ and

His bodily resurrection is a requirement for salvation. When a person has this faith he becomes a Christian. That is why no one can prove God's existence, although you can see results of His power everywhere!' "

The young man had a look of skepticism.

I held my hand in the air. "I asked my instructor to examine his hand," I continued, "how the fingers are of different lengths—then how they fold together the same length so we can grasp things to work and take care of ourselves. Look at your hand. Think of how it works. Think of the wonders of the skin, the circulatory system, the digestive system, the nervous system, not to mention all the other remarkable wonders of the human body and life."

I pointed to the couch. "You could lie on that couch and go mulberries trying to explain logically the origin of what you see in the makeup of your hand. The human mind can't fathom it all. The human mind can't grasp some things—for instance, something with no beginning—"

He interrupted, "Yes, I know. We can't imagine anything without a beginning or end."

Nervously he grabbed a cigarette and lit it. I could see a seed of the gospel had been planted firmly. Someone else would do the watering. The room was full of people, so I changed the subject.

Once again, the Lord had caused me to be a witness. After I had witnessed to my instructor for several months, he admitted there is a Creator. He also was exposed to the doctrine of personal salvation and Pentecostal Christianity—which he'd never heard of before.

On a train trip that I was taking for relaxation, a

young man who had been reading a book about the trial of the Chicago Seven struck up a conversation with me. He must have been about 20 years old and he took the initiative to talk to me. We started by talking about allergies, but within a few minutes he told me he was an atheist and I was witnessing to him.

Afterward I thought about it in amazement. *Why would that young fellow want to talk to a middle-aged lady such as me? How had the opportunity to share the Lord opened so easily when, because of the tiredness of my body, I didn't even have the slightest desire to "collar" somebody and witness?*

Sharing the gospel with strangers is exciting and fulfilling. I've had many of these experiences. Yet most of those I have won to the Lord haven't been strangers that I collared and brought to repentance within 5 minutes. When I was young I used to think that was the most effective way of witnessing, but the majority of those I have had a part in bringing to God were people I had witnessed to and prayed for day in and day out for weeks and months. A large number were young people I won through youth services or Sunday school. In most cases, I wasn't the only person involved in the conversion.

Once God used me to help bring a young girl to Him whose mother had just died of cancer. She didn't even thoroughly understand salvation, but in only a few weeks she found Him as her personal Saviour. Previously, her goal in life had been to become a waitress and sit around on bar stools during breaks and smoke cigarettes. I became her friend and witnessed to her during the week and she got saved during a church service I had urged her to attend.

Another time, it was a teenage boy I contacted by doing visitation for the Sunday school. His sister had visited the class but she wasn't home when my student helper and I went to call on her. We talked to her brother instead and invited him to come. He was in Sunday school the next week. A few Sundays later he knelt at the altar and received the glorious experience of salvation and was baptized in the Holy Spirit. Later his sister accepted Christ too.

I was instrumental in the conversion of another young man who visited my class at another student's invitation, then became interested in one of my girl students. Over a period of more than a year, I encouraged him to give his life to Christ by showing him friendship and always contacting him when he was absent. He had a background in another church that didn't teach total surrender to God. By his actions, he insisted that he was all right spiritually yet I saw in him rebellion toward the Lord and a serious attraction to the world.

I prayed for him almost daily, as I did most of my pupils. One Sunday morning in class we were role-playing witnessing situations. I asked him to play the part of the Christian who was trying to win his barber—an unhappy gentleman who was contemplating suicide because his marriage was breaking up.

Sam (not his real name) liked debate and was good at it. The boy who volunteered to be the barber wasn't a Christian and presented pretty good arguments against becoming one.

During his argument, Sam gave such a challenge to his unsaved opponent in the simulated witnessing encounter that I could feel the sincerity he felt as he told of the advantages of giving one's life completely to Christ.

That night Sam went to the altar. The other young fellow also went. A few months later, Sam received the baptism in the Holy Spirit. He was never the same. He opened his life to the gifts of the Spirit and from then on the total desire of his life was to please God. Today he is active in one of our churches and living a dedicated Christian life.

Sometimes all it takes is scriptural teaching and paying attention to a young person to get him to turn to the Lord. A young man who was interested in journalism was in one of my Sunday school classes. Mike seemed impressed by everything I said—probably because I was a newspaper reporter.

In class I did some in-depth teaching on our church's beliefs and gave the pupils assignments to report on some of our teachings. Mike did very well on his assignments.

When it came time for the annual Christmas play, I suggested Mike for an important role.

"He's not even a Christian!" somebody exclaimed.

I hadn't attended that church very long and didn't know him well. I was shocked. During class he appeared so interested. I could sense his admiration for me, but I felt there was more than a student-teacher relationship. My being a reporter couldn't have kept him nearly spellbound week after week.

"Ask Mike's parents if anything has happened in his spiritual life lately," I said to the Christmas play director.

When she inquired, she found Mike had recently given his life to Christ, his rebellion was over, and he was a different person. Today he is an evangelist.

Witnessing through the church isn't nearly as sensational as some other forms of winning the lost, but after observing the growth of new Christians, I believe it is the most profitable. It is wonderful to point someone to the Lord and have him accept Christ in the home, on the job, or on the street. But for the new Christian to grow spiritually he must become part of a particular flock (church) with a pastor-shepherd. Babes in Christ have to be cared for. The church and Christian fellowship are as necessary to the new Christian as a mother and home are to a new baby.

One young fellow, who had given me plenty of trouble in one of my Sunday school classes, recently came to preach in the church I now attend. He told the church I had been his teacher and that he'd challenged many of my statements and made jokes of some of the things I had said.

"But I wouldn't be in the ministry if it hadn't been for the patience of Sister Brownell," he said.

My face grew hot. My heart began pounding and my throat was tight. It wasn't me who had put him where he was; it was God. He also had parents who had prayed and served the Lord. A feeling of fear enveloped me. If I had influenced his life in only a small way to help him find victorious living through Christ and sacrificial dedication to Him, was I doing that for others?

It's a massive responsibility to be able to influence souls for this life and for eternity. It's when we've seen the Holy Spirit use us to influence others, to change their lives and destinies, that we fully realize the power at our disposal. As with the pilot of a huge passenger jet, what we do affects others. We can help others gain eternal life in heaven or we can help bring about their eternal destruction.

Today I pray: "Lord, keep the fire in my soul burning for You so that others will come to You. May my life be like the watered garden Isaiah prophesied about: 'And the Lord shall guide thee continually, and satisfy thy soul in drought, and make fat thy bones: and thou shalt be like a watered garden, and like a spring of water, whose waters fail not' (Isaiah 58:11)."

9

By This Shall All Men Know

Some of my ideas about real Christianity have had to be changed.

The beginning of this change came when I was a teenager and my parents bought a television set. To me, television was the same as a movie and all my life I'd heard preachers who gave the idea that anyone who attended a theater was a sinner. (Actually, I must have erroneously thought a minister's words when he preached were as divinely inspired as the Word of God.)

The pastor and many church members had televisions, but that didn't bother me like it did when Mom and Dad bought one. At first, I was horrified; then I was humiliated. I'd been pretty liberal with my witnessing, especially when I was invited to do something I didn't believe in doing. Only a year or two earlier, I'd been out riding with a bunch of young people who took me to a drive-in theater against my will. I'd kept my head down during the entire movie so I wouldn't be "defiled" by it.

When my parents purchased a television, a gnawing feeling began in the pit of my stomach that remained for months. I kept thinking, *If we can be wrong about movies, then it's possible we're wrong about other things. How can we tell what is actually a sin when the Bible doesn't have a definite "thou shalt not" about it?*

This gnawing feeling drove me to the Word. I studied night and day, and this study helped me mature as a Christian and realize that basic Pentecostal doctrine agrees with the Word.

About the same time, changes were taking place in the church that related to many people's ideas on holiness. Some people, including me, thought of holiness mostly as outward adorning of the body—especially of women. Some stressed that it didn't matter what you had on the outside, the important thing was the condition of the heart. The other group maintained that if a person had holiness in his heart, it was sure to show up on the outside. I was one of the latter.

All my life I thought you could tell how close to God a woman was by the way she adorned her body. If she was spiritual, she wore very modest clothing, little jewelry, no makeup, and, most often, an old-fashioned hairdo. My gauge for the spirituality of an entire church was based partly on how the women looked.

As I studied the Bible, I realized there was something wrong with my views on spirituality, holiness, and worldliness. But my answer didn't come in a day or a month. It was years before I completely realized where my theology was in error.

The Word substantiated some of my views on the adorning of the body. But what women wore had only very little to do with spirituality, worldliness, and holiness. Actually the "don'ts" of the Bible weren't nearly as important as the "dos"!

First, I discovered that what other people do is actually little of my business. Judging is as bad a sin as immodesty, so that takes care of that.

Much of my learning came from 1 Corinthians 8 where the apostle Paul discusses whether or not it's all right to eat meat sacrificed to idols. This controversy in the Early Church was similar to what happened in my day concerning outward appearance and owning a television. Some people wanted to force their convictions on others in Paul's time, just as I had wanted to do.

As I studied the Word, it also began to dawn on me that outward appearance or whether or not a person has a T.V. isn't the number one test for spirituality. I thought the things you didn't do were what made people know you were a Christian.

I found the answer in John 13:34, 35. Shortly before His arrest and crucifixion, Jesus said: "A new commandment I give unto you, That ye love one another; as I have loved you, that ye also love one another. *By this shall all men know that ye are my disciples, if ye have love one to another.*" Love is the most important, but the way I'd been condemning people who didn't fit into my mold was anything but love!

I don't know why my thinking had become so warped. I saw love in action in my home church while I was growing up as people prayed for one another until the wee hours of the morning and sometimes all night. I saw love in action at home. Not only was there love shown to the members of our family, but we showed love through hospitality and in ministering to others.

I'll never forget one lonely lady my mom used to

visit who had something wrong with her physically that caused her to be unable to lift her head or swallow her saliva. That lady called Mom on the telephone nearly every day and couldn't even talk clearly. Yet Mom dropped everything and took time to share the Word and encourage the old woman. She often visited her. Once I went with Mom, and looking at the continuous string of saliva from the sick lady's mouth made me sick.

I've learned that worldliness is not the way we dress but an attitude by which we govern our lives. If I'm too caught up with my possessions, my family, my job, my appearance, or continuously having a good time, I am worldly and the Bible condemns it.

By the same token, holiness is putting God first and desiring to please Him more than anything else. The dictionary describes holiness as "devoted to the service of God." If we are totally devoted to God, we can enjoy possessions, family, a job, and having an attractive appearance. It is where we put the emphasis that counts. We should put the emphasis on seeking God first, then we can enjoy the other things He gives us (Matthew 6:33).

Emphasis is where I discovered I was wrong. Modesty and separation from the world does have a part in the Christian walk. So does visiting the sick, winning the unsaved to Christ, giving to the poor, and being a friend to the lonely.

To condemn a person for not doing these last four things is practically unheard of. I've never heard a Christian remark, "That person has never won a soul to Jesus, so he can't be spiritual."

Condemnation wasn't the answer in the old days and it isn't the answer now. Condemnation brings us only closed minds, but *love* opens hearts so God can bring salvation and spiritual growth to those who need it.

It would be nice if love were a spiritual *gift* instead of a fruit of the Spirit. Growing fruit is work. But God has seen fit to make us work at love. Frost comes, weeds choke it, there may be a spiritual drought, but if we're persistent there's bound to be a good crop eventually. And that love will show we are His disciples.

10

If It Were Not So

The phone rang. My sister's emotional voice quivered as she spoke. "The nurse said everyone had better get down to the hospital right away. Mom's dying."

My husband and I got in the car and rushed to the hospital. When we arrived, however, my father and other relatives were leaving the hospital. "She's already gone," they told me.

Grief came like a tidal wave. I cried hard.

It was at my sister's home a few minutes later that my brother Everette, a minister, began talking to those of us gathered there. He quoted John 14:1-3:

> Let not your heart be troubled: ye believe in God, believe also in me. In my Father's house are many mansions: if it were not so, I would have told you. I go to prepare a place for you. And if I go and prepare a place for you, I will come again, and receive you unto myself; that where I am, there ye may be also.

Everette paused a minute. "Do you believe it?" he asked. "Now's the time to find out."

He didn't say any more. It seemed very strange to me that he would say such a thing. My father and all eight of us children professed to be born-again Christians. Yet I noticed Everette had a kind of peace about him that I didn't have.

Most of us had a difficult time eating. The law had been laid down by somebody—I don't know whom—that no matter how we felt we were not to display our grief in front of Dad.

It was while we were seated at the table and they told how my aunt, who is a beautician, had gone to the mortuary to fix Mother's hair, that I became unable to control myself. My aunt had fixed Mother's hair for years without charging her because with a large family and a low income my parents couldn't afford any luxury. I knew how much Mother had appreciated my Aunt Marge's generosity. This final act of love—so Mother's beautiful red hair would be fixed the way she always wore it—made me remember how much Mother appreciated each thing anyone did for her. But now she couldn't say thanks!

As soon as I burst into tears, I was led from the room and told to "get a hold of myself." After this gentle reprimand, I buried my grief deep inside me, I didn't go when they picked out the casket. The evening we visited the mortuary, the muscles in my throat were so tight I could hardly swallow.

I remembered Everette's voice saying, "Do you believe it? Now's the time to find out."

I was almost to the casket, following the others as they filed by, when the sickening dread in my stomach changed to a stirring of joy. Suddenly I knew I believed it! As I looked on the face of the shell my mother had used during her earthly stay, I knew she was not there—she was in heaven!

Sure I still loved those wrinkled, work-worn hands. And I still loved those lips that used to gently caress my cheek. But those hands and those lips were not Mama. Mama was gone. She had already seen the Lord and was safely in heaven!

I stood there looking at her earthly body from a distance while the others walked by. I shed no tears. Yet my buried grief had vanished. All I could think of was what Mother probably was doing at that moment. I thought of her meeting Moses and Mary and the apostle Paul and renewing acquaintance with her friends who had preceded her to heaven.

Like a supersonic jet undergoing its first test flight, my faith had been tested. Sure, I've missed Mother. But I know she's in heaven.

11

A Prepared Place

I live on a hill where at night by walking only half a block I can see the mammoth valley of lights that is metropolitan Denver. Often I have stood watching the scene and become nearly overwhelmed with emotion as I realize the valley is full of homes, each with its own problems.

By looking at statistics, I know many people are going through a divorce. Some parents are concerned about rebellious children. A vast number of the people in the valley are enslaved by alcohol or drugs. Many are suffering from pain and disease. Some know they have only a short time to live. Others live in deep poverty and wonder where their next meal is coming from.

Heartache, grief, and pain have been part of life since sin entered the world. The afflictions of man are universal. Death stalks all mankind and eventually gets his prey.

The apostle Paul was aware of the plight of man: "The whole creation groaneth and travaileth in pain together until now . . . waiting for . . . the redemption of our body" (Romans 8:22, 23).

Creation is not without hope. Hope came right after the fall of man. God cursed the serpent who deceived

Eve and He promised redemption through her seed (Genesis 3:15). The result of that redemption is eternal life in heaven through the Lord Jesus Christ.

It is not difficult for me to imagine heaven—beauty, peace, joy, riches, no sorrow, no pain, and no dying or crying. Heaven will more than fulfill all my earthly dreams.

But what about the people who don't make heaven? The Bible describes the place where those who die without accepting Christ go as being filled with unquenchable flames, torture, torment, weeping, wailing, and gnashing of teeth.

I believe in hell as a literal place. Biblical evidence in Matthew 10:28 and Revelation 20:15 is enough for me. And there are many other Scripture passages to substantiate a belief in everlasting punishment for the wicked. Rarely, however, do I think of hell. In fact, my mind can scarcely comprehend the horror of what it must be like. And to think, like heaven, those who go to hell will reside there throughout eternity—forever and ever!

Recently I was wondering about my inability to grasp the reality of eternal hell and the distinct possibility that some of my friends and perhaps a few relatives may spend eternity there. (Oh, my sorrow at the thought!)

I wondered, *Why am I unable to comprehend eternal hell when I can comprehend eternal heaven, even when mentally and doctrinally I believe in both?* Then I remembered that the glories of heaven are a special revelation to the believer by the Holy Spirit. Isaiah wrote (before the Holy Spirit came to dwell in the hearts of men): "For since the beginning of the world men have not heard, nor perceived by the ear, neither hath the eye seen, O God, besides thee, what he hath prepared for him that waiteth for him" (Isaiah 64:4).

After Pentecost, however, Paul quoted Isaiah and then added: "But God hath *revealed* them unto us by his Spirit: for the Spirit searcheth all things, yea the deep things of God" (1 Corinthians 2:10).

It is a special privilege, then, to comprehend heaven, even though we don't know exactly what it will be like.

"Will we play basketball in heaven?" a teenager asked in one of my Sunday school classes. "It wouldn't be any fun," he added, "because every play would be perfect."

"What we do in heaven," I answered, "will be so much better than what we've done here that we won't even miss such things as basketball. When you began growing up did you miss your rattles and toy cars? Heaven will be the realization of everything we've dreamed of here on earth, just as being an adult is the fulfilled dream of childhood."

Things such as clothing, for example, may be simple. My mother dreamed of heaven once and in the dream her clothing was similar to a flower petal—soft, fresh, and needing no care. When she woke up she was rubbing the sheet between her fingers, trying to remember the beauty and softness.

While it is valuable to comprehend eternal hell as far as our soul-winning ministry is concerned, I'd rather comprehend heaven because I'm planning on going there through the redemptive power of our Lord Jesus Christ. We can be purified through the hope of heaven (1 John 3:2, 3). When life gets rough, as it can, we can remember the hope and expectation of tomorrow: "And God shall wipe away all tears . . . ; and there shall be no more death, neither sorrow, nor crying, neither shall there be any more pain: for the former things are passed away" (Revelation 21:4).

12

To Be a Virtuous Woman

The most important assignment I've ever been given is to be a virtuous woman. To live up to Solomon's description of a virtuous woman (Proverbs 31:10-31) seems impossible. But having the *desire* to be a godly wife and mother helps me strive for perfection, which the Lord said we should do.

I remember Rev. Clyde King's interpretation of the Scripture passage: "Be ye therefore perfect, even as your Father which is in heaven is perfect" (Matthew 5:48). Brother King was our pastor for several years when we lived in Pueblo, Colorado, and he said, "We should be perfect in *desire*." If we constantly strive for perfection, we will grow spiritually.

Being a good parent or a good wife takes work, dedication, and trust in God. I've found being in close communion with God is the most important thing we can do to help solve problems in the home.

Years ago when my own parents began attending the church in Fruita to see what had happened to my sister Marjorie, one of the things that impressed them was that the church taught children to obey their parents and that salvation made even teenagers easier to get along with.

I thank God for the church. It helps us rear our

children so that they will take the right path. We seldom miss a service and I've found, as a result, the church means as much to our children as it does to us. It is understood at our house that everyone goes to church, and we've never had a child rebel against our philosophy. If we did, we'd make him go anyway.

Many of the problems Christians have with their children begin (I have often observed) when they allow them to stay home from the house of God. I believe the church is an all-important part of family life and no one should stay home from regular services without ample reason.

The world is making a bid for my children, as well as everyone else's. We as parents constantly need to be aware of what is happening in our children's lives. When we see the world begin to move in, we must act immediately—not wait until an almost irreversible impression or decision has been made.

We've come to the crossroads time and time again where we've needed divine wisdom and much prayer to keep Satan from luring our children onto the broad road leading to destruction. Each time the Lord has answered and they were victorious over the tempter.

I remember when our oldest son, Gary, was in junior high school and I attended one of his concerts. Gary plays both the trumpet and the bass guitar, but the bass guitar is *his* instrument. At the concert, I realized how good he was on the bass and how much he enjoyed playing it. The music seemed to be a part of him. Instead of pride, I felt fear. I lay awake most of the night praying that God would keep him from selling his talent to Satan. And I kept praying.

Several months later, Gary received a telephone call from a man. I was curious to see who had called.

"Oh," Gary explained, "he just insisted that I join his son's group that plays in night clubs on weekends. He said I could easily earn $50 a weekend."

"What did you say?"

"No," he answered. "Told him I play in a group at church." Gary laughed. "Besides, you wouldn't let me."

"Would you play if we'd let you?"

"No." He grinned sheepishly. "I get these offers all the time. Several people have asked me to join their groups."

Gary could play by ear and by notes, so I knew his playing would be in demand. How I thanked God our son had made his own decision to reserve his talents for the Lord's use!

Our children have given their lives to the Lord and we are thankful. To have one's entire family walking with the Lord is the most important blessing in this life.

With God helping us, we can succeed as parents. Each day I find I neglected something I should have done for my children—or I did something I shouldn't have. I see my imperfections. But the Lord gives strength—which helps me keep trying. The Lord also answers prayer. That is the life preserver that can keep parents afloat.

Not only has knowing the Lord helped me to be a better mother, it has helped me be a better wife. As a wife, I have felt the pressures of the world. Our society today doesn't teach submission of the wife to the husband, as the Bible does (1 Peter 3), and periodically I begin thinking about my "rights" and that causes conflict in our home. When I bristle like sandpaper, sparks are bound to fly.

I attended a secular meeting a few years ago to hear a woman who spoke for about 5 minutes on her topic, then preached women's liberation for the rest of her speech. Although I agreed with very little of what she said, her words stuck in my brain.

"Try turning around what men do to you. Would you dare talk to men the way they talk to you? No! Would you dare treat men the way they treat you? No!"

On and on she went. She was a member of a national women's liberation group and knew how to present her views to her audience. Other women at the meeting that night cheered and yelled agreement as she spoke.

Much attention has been focused on women being mistreated by men and, in most cases, I think the American home is made unhappier by it. God did not create women to be the heads of their households. Men were made to make the major decisions, taking the final responsibility for their wives and families. With so much attention on women's rights, however, it's easy to forget that God knew what He was doing when he set up the government of the home.

Once when I felt I was being mistreated because my opinion on a certain matter was completely ignored and unappreciated, I became almost willing to sacrifice my marriage for women's rights. I had a good cry because it appeared my husband didn't think I was as smart as he was. He had made a decision and nothing I could say would change his mind. After I threw my tantrum, I drove out to the country where wheat fields fanned in the wind. Looking at the peaceful mountains in the background helped calm my turbulent spirit.

When I returned home, however, there was an urgent, almost compelling force that made me want to pack my suitcase, take all my children, and leave my husband. I kept trying to reason with myself, knowing that what had happened was a silly reason for getting so upset and leaving. The drive to leave him became more urgent, however, and was almost like something was physically pushing me to go pack my clothes.

Suddenly I knew this was something beyond my own emotions. "Satan, I rebuke you in the name of Jesus!" I exclaimed. Immediately a calmness swept over me. The next morning when I awoke in my own bed, with circumstances the same as they had been the previous day but with my own bitterness resolved, I thanked the Lord I had not submitted to Satan.

That was several years ago, and I still thank God I stayed with my husband and that we have power over the enemy through Jesus Christ.

We have had problems, as all married couples do, but God has made our marriage beautiful. Sometimes we can go months at a time without having a serious argument. When we do get angry with one another, we make it a policy to not let the sun go down on our wrath (Ephesians 4:26).

In our 25 years, the Lord has made our marriage a deep, satisfying, romantic relationship. I love Les so much that often I need only to touch him to feel calm and gain strength.

Solomon's description of a virtuous woman and Peter's summary of the attributes of holy women (1 Peter 3) challenge me to be a better wife and mother. I long to obtain the spirit that Peter says is of great price in the sight of God (v. 4). (With all the wealth

God has, it must *really* be valuable.) Solomon said the price of a virtuous woman is far above rubies.

I hope that my husband trusts in me and that I will do him good and not evil all the days of his life. I intend to look well to the ways of my household and eat not the bread of idleness. With God's help I can perform my duties as a godly wife and mother. Above everything, I must not cease to fear the Lord but to continually follow the guidance of the Scriptures and the Holy Spirit.

As I have walked with the Lord this far, I see His hand of blessing. He has helped us rear children who love and serve Him. (We're not through rearing them yet, but today they love God and we have faith for the future.) He has made our marriage a wonderful thing as we serve the Lord together and our love for one another grows as a giant sequoia tree—solid, secure, and breathtaking.

Come to think of it, a virtuous woman shouldn't be called blessed—it should be the Lord! If I ever really succeed at my assignment of being a virtuous woman, the glory will be *His*.

13

Attacked

The figure of a sloppily dressed young person approached us as we walked to our car in downtown Denver after an Andrae Crouch concert sponsored by Youth for Christ. I clutched my purse in front of me, locking it against me with both arms, preparing to pass the suspicious-looking individual.

A slight glance told me the character was a short young man about 20 or 21 years old, wearing round wire-rimmed glasses, and his sandy hair in a ponytail. The crouched way he darted about on the sidewalk caused a feeling of fear to rise up inside me.

Suddenly he took a giant step toward me. Carolyn, my daughter who was walking with me, later said he spat a nasty glob of saliva toward me, but the cool breeze caused it to miss the target. I thought he was lunging for my purse and neatly sidestepped his sweep toward me.

He stepped back after his lunge, then resumed walking toward us. As soon as he was beside me, he ran at me, grabbed my upper torso, tightly pinning my arms at my sides, while wrapping his feet around my legs.

I guess I should have fallen, but I stood. My head was ducked down and my arms were still at my waist, holding my purse. The impact made me think the whole thing had been done just to frighten me, because my attacker didn't have the strength I'd anticipated.

The struggle, however, became more fierce as the seconds passed. It seemed the attacker's feet were now on the ground and I was going to be taken somewhere—or else knocked off my feet.

A bone-scraping scream pierced the air. I knew it was Carolyn. Something clicked in my mind. I'd always read that during an attack, a woman should scream her lungs out, and fight with everything she has.

Carolyn's screams continued, spontaneous and echoing among the brick buildings, cement, and pavement of downtown Denver. I began to scream also, and I got one hand loose and to the back of my assailant's neck. I dug my fingernails in, then came around to the face, ripped off the glasses, and began scratching at the eyes and face.

I was released. The attacker looked up and down the street quickly to see who was coming as a result of our screams. Several young girls and one man were running toward us.

My assailant looked as if he'd decided to attack again as he stood there half-crouched, hands outstretched, eyeing me.

"Help us, Jesus!" I screamed so loudly I probably was heard for three blocks. My cry must have reached the portals of heaven also, for my assailant turned and fled.

Carolyn and I ran in the opposite direction. As I ran, my heart pounding and my breath coming in gasps, I realized I couldn't see—my glasses were gone.

"There's a police station across the street!" Carolyn exclaimed between sobs.

"Where?" I panted. I couldn't see that far.

"Shall we go there?" she asked.

"Yes!" I exclaimed, and she led the way.

We ran into the station and leaned across the high front desk—Carolyn still sobbing hysterically; me panting and shaking like a person with palsy.

"Can I help you?" the officer inquired calmly.

For a few moments we couldn't speak. My throat was dry and sore from screaming. I finally got the story out and Carolyn became calm enough to give the officers a detailed description of my attacker.

The desk sergeant radioed an officer in the area. Two other policemen came to take information from us, and they took me to where I'd been attacked and helped me find my glasses. We also found the lens from my assailant's glasses.

Before we got back to the station, a plain-clothed detective met us.

"We've got the suspect," he announced, "but it's a female, not a male."

The officers led us to an elevator where two men stood on both sides of the most pitiful-looking young lady I've ever seen. I was almost ashamed at how I'd fought her. A streak of blood was on the cheek turned our way. "Is this the person who attacked you?" an officer asked.

"I think so," I answered. The clothes were the same, the hair was the same, but I hadn't had a good look at the face before. "Does she look like the person to you?" I asked Carolyn.

"Yes," Carolyn said. "She's the one."

As the girl stood staring straight ahead as if we

weren't there, I couldn't help comparing her to my lovely, talented, dedicated Christian daughter beside me. Love began filling me as I looked at that broken piece of humanity—dirty; the shabby man's clothing extremely large on her small body; her acne-covered face set with rebellion and hate.

It seemed strange that the police officers left her before us in silence for so long. I felt I should say something.

"I'm sorry this had to happen," I said, trying to reach out to her in spite of my pressing charges and putting her in jail. "But when you think no one else in the whole world loves you, remember Jesus loves you."

The elevator doors closed and an officer directed us to another room.

I was shocked when the girl called me a few weeks later from the jail.

"I'm getting mighty tired of sitting in jail," she said. I could hear a lot of noise in the background and someone talking over a loud speaker. "I want to know if you'll drop the charges."

"I hate to make you stay in jail," I said, fear beginning to pump through my veins, "but I don't think I should send you out on the streets to do the same thing to someone else. Why did you attack me?"

How has she obtained my name and address? I kept thinking.

"I kept passing people on the street who were high on God or something," she answered. "I could feel this *energy* coming out of them. I couldn't stand it. I had to do something."

As I continued talking with her, some of what she

said didn't make sense. But she had one goal in mind, which she made clear.

"Will you drop the charges?" she asked again and again.

During the end of the conversation, my children began making noise in the kitchen.

"Do you have small children?" she asked. "I can hear them in the background. Are you going to drop the charges?"

Suddenly I felt as if she were threatening me. I didn't tell her I had small children.

"I'll pray about it and think about it some more," I said, trying not to let her know how much I was beginning to shake.

When I hung up the phone, I became completely cold. I trembled from head to toe. When I told my husband the girl had my name and address, I said, "Maybe we'd better move!"

As each second ticked by, fear reached another height, until I was in panic. I called the associate pastor of our church, who is a former Denver policeman, and had him pray with me.

Although the panic subsided, fear plagued me for several hours. I decided to fast and pray one meal a day for 3 days (all I can usually do and keep up with the demands of my large family), so that if I ever had another encounter with the young woman I would be strong enough spiritually to be able to withstand the satanic power that seemed to be driving her. That week, my fear finally left me.

Later the district attorney contacted me and asked if the girl would take psychiatric treatments for a year, would I agree to not go to court. I agreed. I didn't want to go to court anyway. And I knew the girl might get off without a lengthy jail term even if I did.

About a year later, the DA sent me a check from my assailant in restitution for my broken glasses and the necessary doctor's services (in the event I had been injured internally).

If I were to believe what she told me—that she attacked me because of spiritual "energy"—this was my first experience with real religious persecution.

Whether or not that was her motive, Satan is warring with Christians today. He would like to drive people to spit on the Lord's children, fill them with fear, and even take their lives.

Christians in other countries are suffering every day. Someday this may happen in the United States. Years ago a number of evangelists preached that religious persecution would come to America. This was during the years when many new homes contained bomb shelters and citizens everywhere feared Communism was going to take over our country.

Today our country allows Communists to preach their ideals openly and Communist newspapers are as available to university students as the daily city newspaper. No longer are we building bomb shelters —for the Communists don't seem to be coming with bombs but with textbooks, law books, and newspapers. (Many anti-God laws that interfere with spreading the gospel and God's Word exist without the Communists.) But suppose, whatever the weapons, Communists took over our country. Would I be willing to die for Jesus Christ?

Years ago, the evangelists who preached those hair-straightening sermons on religious persecution, asked that question. The audience responded with a unanimous, "Yes!" and went to the altar *en masse.*

I went too, but I kept thinking, *Lord I really don't know.* At the time I was safely in a church with friends. I was not in pain. My children weren't being tortured. How could I really say, when the possibility is so remote, that I am willing to die for the Lord?

Peter, I remembered, had said he was ready to die for his Master, but he backed down to an unarmed maiden.

Jesus said when persecution comes, to "take no thought how or what ye shall speak: for it shall be given you in that same hour what ye shall speak. For it is not ye that speak, but the Spirit of your Father which speaketh in you" (Matthew 10:19, 20).

I pray the Rapture takes place before any more of God's people have to suffer persecution. However, if we do have to die for the sake of the gospel, Jesus will be there, standing at the right hand of God, ready to receive our souls as He did Stephen's in the Book of Acts. If the crisis comes, God has already promised to give us words to speak and peace in our souls. Jesus also said concerning persecution: "Be not afraid of them that kill the body, and after that have no more that they can do. But I will forewarn you whom ye shall fear: Fear him, which after he hath killed hath power to cast into hell; yea, I say unto you, Fear him" (Luke 12:4, 5).

In my time of crisis when the young woman attacked me, the Lord was there. When I screamed the name of Jesus she ran. It was strange that when we took off in the opposite direction from the way she went, we didn't meet the man who had been running to help us, his suit coat flapping in the wind. Carolyn and I both noticed, when we later reflected on the experience, that it was strange that we didn't meet or see him or the teenage girls as we ran their way. Had God sent angels to our aid?

Whatever the case, I've learned that God will be with us in any situation. Such a fact is easy to see as we look at the past. What we need is faith to see that His continuing presence and power is a fact of the future.

14

My Choice

Being a Christian is an extremely personal matter. No one can obtain salvation for another. Each person has to believe in God and accept Christ for himself.

My choice to be a Christian isn't merely because of my background. I have *chosen* to be a follower of Jesus Christ. Basic to being a Christian is my belief in God as Creator—infinite, eternal, holy, merciful, and loving. He is also the Source of moral law and is the Righteous Judge.

I came about my belief in God partly because I was reared in a Christian home, yes. In my late teens, however, I was plagued by doubts. My faith wasn't solid. Those who challenged the existence of God caused fear to rise up within me.

Because of this fear, I began to study God's Word and investigate the basis of my faith. I found evolution and atheism take more faith than Christianity. I have seen no evidence that monkeys are changing into humans now or ever have. I see no evidence that any species is changing or has changed into another. Each reproduces after its kind as the Bible says God designed it to do. (Cross-reproduction produces a hybrid, which is sterile.) After life, all flesh returns to dust, from whence the Book of Genesis says it came.

To me, the perfection of Creation is evidence that there is a Designer who is much greater than man. I *choose* to believe the Designer is God.

I also believe that a Creator who made a world such as ours would be interested in communicating with His creation, and I believe God communicates with man—His highest creation—through His Word, through His servants, and by His Spirit.

I have communicated with God. He has spoken to me through His Word, ministers, other Christians, and the utterance gifts of the Holy Spirit. He has spoken to me by His Spirit—not audibly, but clearly enough for me to know He has spoken.

Once when I was very discouraged with my work as a writer, God spoke to me three nights in a row through Scripture passages that applied to my situation. The first was encouragement; the second, a command for obedience; and, the third, a promise for God's help in my work.

That God actually cared and was concerned about my work and my problems, even though compared to other problems in the world mine seemed insignificant, was both encouraging and frightening. I wouldn't have felt any different about it if God had given me a vision or I'd heard Him speak audibly. I *know* God gave me those Scripture passages as a message from Him and they changed my attitude toward my writing ministry.

In addition to a basic belief in God and His Word, the Christian must believe in the Lord Jesus Christ and the *fact* of His resurrection. This belief also is extremely personal.

Sometimes we begin to think that the present generation of scoffers and unbelievers is something new.

It's not. In the story Jesus told of the rich man and Lazarus, the rich man asked Abraham to send Lazarus back from the dead to warn his relatives about hell (Luke 16:30, 31).

"If they hear not Moses and the prophets," Abraham said, "neither will they be persuaded, though one rose from the dead."

That truth was verified when many refused to believe in the resurrection of the Lord Jesus Christ.

I choose to believe in the Resurrection because: (1) if Jesus *was* the Son of God, His resurrection was to be expected; (2) His life, death, and resurrection were a fulfillment of Biblical prophecies written by many writers hundreds of years before His birth; (3) His disciples (with the exception of John and Judas) gave their lives for their belief in His resurrection; and (4) He is at the right hand of the Father answering prayer, interceding, and sending the Comforter, the Holy Spirit, *today* as He said He would when He went away.

I not only *choose* to be a Christian, I am also convinced that being a Christian is the only way to live. True, I have not been a Buddhist, a follower of Islam, or an atheist, but I have observed that Christianity is the only religion that puts a song in the heart. I sing in a gospel singing group, but the song in my heart was there years before there was a group called "Damascus Singers." Sometimes just thinking about the things of the Lord causes me to break forth in singing—such as the time I was serving jury duty and I began thinking how the accusers of a defendant can't touch him without going through his attorney. I remember that Jesus Christ is our Advocate and Satan can't bring accusations against us to the Father without the intervention of our Lord. Right there in my car on the way home I began singing.

More songs have been written about Jesus Christ than any person who ever lived. Down through the ages we have evidence of the joyous song God gives. David wrote of praising the Lord with singing. Charles Wesley penned, "O, for a thousand tongues to sing of my Redeemer's praise!" Martin Luther wrote, "A mighty fortress is our God." Almost without exception Christians sing, as is evidenced in churches and by the abundance of gospel music available.

When Jesus Christ lives in man's heart there is abundant life, whether in a prison (as the life of Watchman Nee testified) or a big American penthouse. In fact, as Howard Hughes showed the world, life—no matter how luxurious—is not really abundant without the Lord.

I've enjoyed abundant life with Jesus. It was just as enjoyable when I lived in a dingy railroad depot years ago and they brought our water in a keg on a motor car, as it is now in my beautiful five-bedroom house in the suburbs of Denver.

Walking in the "light" with the Lord Jesus Christ (1 John 1) is a wonderful way to live. Although we don't know the future, we can see, through the guidance of the Spirit and the Word, a few steps ahead and can take them in faith that He's leading the way.

I would have enjoyed walking physically with Jesus when He was here on earth, as the disciples did. However, I've accepted the Comforter He promised when He went away. Accepting that Comforter makes me a Pentecostal Christian with benefits comparable to those of the Early Church.

I'm so glad I've found this way of life.